BOB
—— THE ——
MONEY
DOUBLER

A kid entrepreneur must Make a Million Dollars
by Doubling a Penny in 30 Days or Else

Mahugu Nuthu

TO ALL YOUNG ASPIRING
ENTREPRENEURS. YOU ARE THE FUTURE
JOB CREATORS.

TABLE OF CONTENTS

THE ORACLE OF THE COPPERS

In his dream, Bob was somewhere so magnificent that he wanted to stay there forever. He was licking a vanilla ice cream cone while relaxing on a sugar-white sandy beach when the Oracle of the Coppers approached him.

The Oracle stretched out his hands and wings dramatically and spoke in a deep voice. "Here's a little gift that's worth a lot."

Bob was stretching his arm out to receive the reddish-brown metal coin. Suddenly, he was jolted to reality by his mom's voice.

"Robert William Benjamin!"

Gosh! There was trouble in paradise! Whenever Mom called him by his full name, Bob knew he was in jeopardy. Hurriedly, he began cleaning his room. He was clearing out under his bed when he saw something shiny. It was as if the copper coin from his dream had just appeared there.

"What in the world?" he wondered. "What are the odds?"

Bob rushed downstairs to tell his family about the dream and the copper coin. The Benjamins lived at Hope Apartments on Maple Avenue. It was a small three-bedroom apartment. Bob had two older brothers who were students at Washington Middle School on Main

Street, Dollarville. Nelson Benjamin ("Nelly") was 11. Edward Benjamin ("Ned") was 13. Bob's mom, Lira, worked as a cashier at a Main Street grocery store. Bob's dad, Benjamin, worked at Dollarville railway yard as a Track Laborer.

"Keep it, Bob. You picked it up, so you'll have all the good luck," Mom opined after Bob excitedly narrated the story. Finding a coin under the bed was usually considered a sign of good fortune.

"Don't forget your mama when you become rich and famous," she added jokingly.

But his brothers took offense with the whole drama. As usual, they thought Bob was just being silly. As the youngest child, he seemed to enjoy all their parents' attention. The kingdom that was once theirs was now ruled by their little brother. Bob often dominated dinner table discussions with his wacky money ideas. To his brothers, Bob was also a total embarrassment. Bob was well known throughout the neighborhood as the kid who likes watching business shows. He was probably the only kid who binge-watched money shows.

"That's a worthless coin. Just throw it away," Nelly snapped.

"Even if you were to give that to anyone, he would think you insulted him," Ned rebuked Bob. Then both his brothers started laughing. It was no secret that Bob, the youngest, loved the spotlight. He was always doing things to get his parents' attention. His brothers loved to tease him and get on his nerves because of that.

"We salute you, Mr. Moneybags," Nelly teased.

"No, Nelly. Mr. Shiny Penny," Ned roared, bursting into a thunderous and mischievous laugh.

Mom did little to stop them. Boys will be boys, and for her, this was just another sibling squabble. "Bob, you are being too sensitive," was Mom's favorite line. However, Bob was hurt by the comments and sadly left the room where his brothers were. Bob could not stop thinking about his million dollar dream. He decided to report the issue to Uncle WalkaWaylen DeMonte who lived in the big city of Denver, 40 miles away. He was the one person who never failed to listen, reassure, or defend him. His positivity was always infectious. Every kid deserves a champion.

Dollarville was a lovely little railroad town east of Denver. Founded in 1879, the tiny Colorado town once served as the main railway depot. Besides the beautiful mountains, forests, and streams, there was a great sense of small town peace and loyalty. The historic Main Street that cuts through Dollarville was home to schools, shops, restaurants, and other businesses. The downtown was filled with cafes, outdoor-apparel boutiques, and eclectic dining. The town also flaunted many beautiful spots in nature, including Silver Run Park. The Rocky Mountains framed the Denver skyscrapers on the west.

Uncle WalkaWaylen DeMonte picked up on the third ring.

"Hi, Uncle Doubler," Bob started, calling WalkaWaylen DeMonte by his nickname. Kids called him Uncle W. or simply Doubler because his name was a little tongue twisting.

"Hello Bob, my favorite nephew, but don't tell anyone I said that" he whispered softly. Bob told Uncle Doubler about his dream, the penny, and what his brothers had said. Bob felt he could always talk to his uncle. His uncle had a way of seeing things his way. He felt that Uncle Doubler was always there for him, and everyone needs someone in their corner.

Uncle Doubler appreciated Bob's curiosity, his discipline with money at such a young age, and good listening skills. He knew Bob's brothers teased him often, and as a 9-year-old, the teasing affected him emotionally. He was tired of having everything swept under the proverbial carpet. He demanded to speak with Ned and Nelly. Uncle Doubler strongly reprimanded Ned and Nelly for their inappropriate behavior when they got on the call.

"Boys, don't you know every million starts with a shiny penny? No? Okay, we'll show you," he threatened.

He then promised to help Bob turn the shiny penny into millions. That would show Ned and Nelly not to laugh at a 9- year-old. All Bob had to do was follow one simple rule: he should double his money for 30 days.

"You can only do this by earning, saving, or investing. For example, you can buy something for $1, and you must resell it at a higher price. If you can't double the money by selling, you must work to earn it."

They both agreed that every day that the money doubles, Bob should call Uncle Doubler. The days did not have to be back -to-back.

"Don't let anyone bring you down," Uncle added. "One day, those two naysayers will fall in line and watch."

He rushed to tell his family, but his brothers did not want to hear the story. He was met with the usual petty jabs. Ned and Nelly were always quick to kill his dreams and squash his ideas.

"Whatever!" Ned yelled as he stomped his foot and balled his fists up in anger. "Baloney! That's the stupidest thing I've ever heard," Nelly fumed.

"I see it differently. Let's leave it at that," Bob said, disappointed.

But Bob had his supporters too. Mom promised to help if Bob kept his room tidy. Dad promised to help if Bob stayed in school and maintained good grades. Uncle Noah, Uncle James, and Aunt Sophia pledged to help with no conditions.

"Thanks, everyone!" It was time to bust a move. Unlike his entitled brothers, Bob had a grateful heart. Bob broke into his happy "Chicken Dance," where he flapped his arms like a chicken. Bob loved to dance. He learned most of his moves from his mom. Bob was a natural dancer. He was able to grasp the skills of dancing with ease at a young age.

Impressed by his ability to feel rhythm and dance seamlessly, Mom encouraged him to try some old school moves. She quickly discovered that Bob had a natural aptitude for movement and a 'feel' for music. Bob's willingness to learn and make changes made it easier for Mom to teach him dancing styles from her younger days.

That night, Bob bought two erasers from his friend for 1 cent, setting his plan in motion.

Bob was determined to make this happen. If Bob failed, Ned and Nelly would laugh at him forever.

Day 1

HOW BOB TURNED 1 CENT INTO 2 CENTS

Bob woke up with a burning desire to prove his brothers wrong. Bob was a student at Hamilton Elementary School on Main Street, Dollarville. After school, he sold the two erasers to his friends in the 4th-grade block. Just like that, Bob now had 2 cents! He jumped up joyfully.

"An extra penny, cha-ching, cha-ching," he murmured to himself. Bob now believed that the Oracle was guiding him. That afternoon, he called Uncle Doubler with the breaking news.

"First doubling complete!" he shouted.

Bob told his uncle about the erasers and how he sold them with glee. Uncle Doubler could hear the excitement and commitment in Bob's voice. He was now hooked on doubling the money.

"Awesome!" Uncle Doubler replied. "You are the real Doubler. You can't control what your brothers do, but you can control your reaction to it."

It was time to celebrate. Bob broke into a little dance known as "The Robot." Dancing always improved his mood.

That evening, with all the family at the table having dinner, he told them what happened. He told the story about selling the erasers, his brown eyes shining brightly. His dad was sitting at the head of the table, munching on the chicken casserole Mom had made while he listened to Bob's story. Mom was preoccupied with Ned and Nelly as she passed them servings of her casserole and milk.

"Big whopping deal," Nelly shrugged as he rolled his eyes at Bob. "How could you be so stupid, Mr. Coppers?"

"One day, I will be a millionaire," Bob replied defiantly. "As Uncle Doubler said, every million starts with a shiny penny." "I'll bet you will when pigs fly!" Ned smirkingly added, showing a glint of his newly polished braces.

"Not in a million years," Nelly added. "Wait. When hell freezes over. Listen, Uncle Doubler is just being nice. There is no way you can make a million from a single penny. You are just a spoiled baby who knows nothing about earning actual money."

"Stay tuned," Bob warned. "Watch this kid."

Their mother, listening to the exchange between her sons, realized that she needed to stop the conversation right now before it went any further.

"How was work today, honey?" she asked her husband. Before their father could answer the question, Ned blurted out to Bob, "You know you're supposed to be doing your homework, right?"

Mom turned toward Bob, her brows wrinkling beneath her curly black hair sprinkled with a few grays. Bob quickly found himself on the receiving end of Mom's death stare.

"Did you finish your homework today, Bob?"

Bob shifted his eyes on his half-eaten chicken casserole. "No, Mom, I am almost finished, though," he replied, feeling deflated. Bob did not like being tattled on by Ned.

"I don't like it when you tell me to do my homework!" he shouted at Ned, holding back tears.

The joy he had felt before from accomplishing that first doubling was no longer there. Bob retired to his room tearful and broken down. But Bob was not giving up. Later that night, Bob used his two cents to buy two more erasers. His friend was pleased to get a return customer.

Day 2

HOW BOB TURNED 2 CENTS INTO 4 CENTS

Bob was ready to close a deal. This day was fueled by those who doubted him. He couldn't wait to put the doubting brothers in their place.

It was against the rules to sell items at Hamilton Elementary School. Teachers did not want kids selling items during class time. It would have been disruptive. Even outside the school, children were supposed to have a parent's consent to make purchases. Bob did not want trouble, so he came up with a clever plan. He did not carry items to school. He made sure the payments did not happen in the school, and the goods stayed at home. He also made sure the parents were involved. Mom and the parents of the other kids were helpful. The kids thought it was fun.

On his way home from school, Bob sold the 4 erasers to his friends for 1 cent each. Bob now had 4 cents. It was a great feeling.

"Hurrah! Hurrah! Hurrah!" Bob cried out, feeling good about his second doubling.

It was time to get locking and dropping. Bob broke into a little dance known as "The Limbo" as he entered their house.

The dance continued in the living room. Bob pretended to go under the stick in front of the TV while his brothers sat on the sofa watching their favorite show. His brothers did not appreciate his celebratory dance moves. It was obvious from their contorted faces. However, Bob was feeling on top of the world, so he did it anyway. Dancing always helped him reduce anxiety.

"Whoop-de-doo. Big deal. Who cares?" Nelly hissed.

Bob still danced without care. He was getting tired of his brothers putting him down, humiliating him around his friends, and making fun of everything about him. Mom would not take it seriously. According to her, the horseplay was typical sibling bickering.

"Oh well, boys will be boys," she would say when Uncle Doubler called specifically about this.

Bob's brothers were not very fond of him. They both thought he was a nuisance. They thought he was too curious and came off as nosy. He asked too many questions, and all that money talk seemed silly and a waste of time. Bob thought Ned and Nelly were envious of his curiosity. But it was not his fault that he was born with a hungry mind.

With all that was going on in the house, Bob almost forgot to call Uncle Doubler. "I'm now at 4 cents!" he told his uncle.

"Bravo! That was fantastic!" Uncle Doubler exclaimed. He knew the importance of having a viable business model.

That evening, after the customers came with their parents to pick the items and deliver cash, Bob bought the last 8 erasers from his friend for a total of 4 cents. The friend told him where he had purchased the erasers, a closing office supply store. Few 4th graders knew about it.

Day 3

HOW BOB TURNED 4 CENTS INTO 8 CENTS

This morning was particularly sweet. The demand was up! The word about Bob's new erasers was getting around. Bob sold the 8 erasers to other children in the classroom next door for 1 cent each. Bob now had 8 cents.

"Yippee!" Bob exclaimed, happy that he was able to maintain his momentum.

It was time to get down. Bob broke into a little dance known as "The Loco-Motion" as he entered his home. He stepped his right leg forward, then his left leg backward, and then did a double step in place with both legs while waving and clapping his hands above his head.

With every cent he earned and celebrated, his brothers became meaner. Bob was tired of their mean behavior. Nevertheless, he was determined to reach his goal. Instead of letting his brothers' mean reactions get to him, he used it as motivation to work harder.

Bob doubled his money yet again. He called Uncle Doubler, his secret weapon.

"Brilliant!" Uncle Doubler rejoiced. He was delighted with his nephew's commitment and progress. He encouraged Bob to keep things going.

This day, the kids did not have to come to Bob's home. Bob and Mom delivered the erasers to all of them and collected the money.

That evening, Bob bought 16 erasers for 8 cents from the closing office supply store that his friend had talked about.

Day 4

HOW BOB TURNED 8 CENTS INTO 16 CENTS

Bob was looking forward to a great day. He hoped to continue his lucky streak. The business was booming, and the day did not disappoint. He had waiting customers.

Bob sold the 16 erasers for 1 cent each. Just like that, Bob now had 16 cents on the way.

"Yay, I'm doing it. I'm doubling!" Bob jumped up with joy.

His older brothers did not appreciate his celebrating and dancing excitedly in front of them once he got home. However, he was too glad to care, so he did it anyway. It was time to take the floor on a serious note.

Bob broke into a little dance known as "Running Man," which involved running in place on the carpet in the dining room entrance. The family was about to sit and have dinner.

He had doubled his money yet again. He called Uncle Doubler.

"Fantastic! I just love it!" he gushed, sounding just as excited as Bob about his achievement.

That evening after delivery, Bob bought 32 erasers for 16 cents.

Day 5

HOW BOB TURNED 16 CENTS INTO 32 CENTS

Bob viewed each day as a challenge to do better. For a moment, he was no longer afraid to become an object of ridicule. But he knew the fear of being laughed at will come back. This day he sold all 32 erasers for 1 cent each. Bob now had 32 cents.

"Sweet!" Bob roared. He felt happy that his venture was working out and that, so far, he had been able to meet his goal of doubling his money daily. A good word from friends was the best source of his customers. Recommendations were essential because they helped potential customers make purchase decisions. The good old word of mouth was his best marketing channel.

As much as Bob was doing well, his brothers' attitude still did not improve. They became meaner. Bob danced anyway. It was time to get rolling.

Bob broke into a little dance known as "Funky Chicken." He was flapping both his arms, with elbows bent, bobbing his head, and moving his legs to an imaginary beat.

He had doubled his money again. He called Uncle Doubler. As usual, his uncle was happy for him. As he hung the phone up, Bob continued with the Funky Chicken dance again, laughing as he danced. His brothers had to leave the room in a hurry.

That evening, Bob bought 64 erasers for 32 cents.

Day 6

HOW BOB TURNED 32 CENTS INTO
64 CENTS

This morning, Bob found a perfectly shaped four-leaf clover while on his way to school. In Dollarville, that was considered the ultimate symbol of luck. He was so busy admiring it he almost stepped on a black cat. He was sure that the cat crossing his path neutralized his luck, but he kept his fingers crossed for the rest of the way.

The day did not disappoint. The four-leaf clover luck was still with him. Bob was able to sell all 64 erasers to his friends for 1 cent each. Bob was now 64 cents rich. "Woohoo!"

He couldn't wait to get home to start popping, locking, dropping, and drilling. Bob decided to celebrate this time by doing an old-school hip-hop dance known as "The Worm." He lay on the floor and started making wavelike movements, using his torso and legs. His little body mimicked a caterpillar's movement.

Bob had doubled his money yet again. He made his now customary earnings call to Uncle Doubler.

"Great! I'm so excited for you!" replied Uncle Doubler. "I am proud that you have found a way to double your money."

This particular day was special. Mom helped him set up a stall in the front yard. It was a "Lemonade Stand" with no food or refreshments. The kid customers came with their parents to pick the items and deliver cash.

Bob was not entirely satisfied with the buying and selling erasers business, though. He felt it was getting old and boring. He wanted to take his business to the next level and make more money before the office supply store closed for good. He was running against time. That evening, Bob reinvested all his money, including the profits. This time he bought 2 pencils for a total of 64 cents. He was going for the coveted $1 milestone.

Day 7

HOW BOB TURNED 64 CENTS INTO $1.28

This day Bob made sure to wear his lucky t-shirt. Everyone wants a little luck in their life. On his way to school, he made sure Ned was not following him or crossing his path. He was worse than a black cat. Ned carried along bad energy. He was a dream killer.

Bob sold the 2 pencils to his friends for 64 cents each. Bob now had $1.28. Making his first dollar was a giant step.

"Boo-yah! Guess who just made a whole dollar?" Bob thundered. "This cash whisperer!"

Bob couldn't contain his excitement! Nonetheless, he tried not to celebrate because he was afraid his brothers would start making mean jokes. Unable to control his feelings, he did it anyway. After all, it was time to get popping, locking, dropping, and sliding.

Bob broke into a little dance known as "Raise the Roof." He pranced around his room, pumping his arms with palms turned up toward the ceiling and giggling with glee.

"Everybody clap your hands!" he shouted as he was entering the living room.

"Bwahahaha!" Nelly laughed mischievously and making the "cuckoo" sign to Ned. They both thought Bob had lost his marbles.

"You want to turn the penny into a million? In your dreams!" Ned responded with maniacal laughter.

"One day, you will beg to live in my dreams." Bob protested. He couldn't wait to prove them wrong.

Uncle Doubler was impressed that Bob was still able to meet his target, even after changing to a new product. "Wow, how about that! Way to go, little man!" exclaimed his uncle.

That evening, Bob bought 4 pencils for $1.28 at the closing office supply store. It was the final day for the store. Bob was sad about it, but he was not a quitter.

Day 8

HOW BOB TURNED $1.28 INTO $2.56

"Rabbit, rabbit, rabbit," Bob shouted before he got out of bed that morning. In Dollarville, the ritual was supposed to bring one good luck for the rest of the day. As the nation's most superstitious city, Dollarville was an exciting place. Black cats were not the only thing that was considered unlucky. Opening an umbrella in the house was bad luck. Dollarville was the only city in America with no "13" or "666" numbers as addresses. There were municipal regulations prohibiting those bad luck numbers.

Bob's family was superstitious, too. Mom carried a lucky $2 bill in her purse. Dad had horseshoes on the wall. There were dream catchers above Ned's bed.

This was not a fun day. Bob needed to find different things to sell and a new supplier. But first things first. He had inventory for the day.

Bob sold the 4 pencils to his schoolmates on his way home for 64 cents each. Bob now had $2.56.

"What a beautiful day!" Bob declared, smiling at how he was able to change a penny into $2.56. It was time to cut a rug.

Bob broke into a little dance known as "The Snake." He was elated. His brothers were not around today to give their customary disdainful looks. They were probably still causing trouble out there, Bob thought.

He had doubled his money. As usual, he called Uncle Doubler. "Marvelous! That's just wonderful," Uncle Doubler remarked.

That evening, Bob followed Mom to a church sale and bought 2 books for a total of $2.56. This was another level for Bob. He was so excited.

Day 9

HOW BOB TURNED $2.56 INTO $5.12

"So far, so good," Bob said to himself, rapping his knuckles on a wooden table. He did not want to jinx his chances.

Bob planned to keep the momentum. His goal was to hit $10 by the end of day. He believed in creating opportunities by working hard for the sales.

This day Bob sold the 2 books from the church sale to his friends for $2.56 each. Bob now had $5.12.

"Nice!" Bob felt motivated more than ever. It had only been a few days, and he had managed it all by himself.

He started making his father's signature move, a little dance known as "The Cabbage Patch." He rocked his shoulders and arms in unison and cabbage-patched around the kitchen.

He had successfully doubled his money with books. As always, he kept his promise and called Uncle Doubler.

"Wow! I love it!" Uncle Doubler exclaimed. "You took the initiative and changed your strategy, and you were still able to double the money."

That evening, Bob was eager to see what he could find to double his money. He followed his mom to a community garage sale and bought 4 books for a total of $5.12.

Day 10

HOW BOB TURNED $5.12 INTO $10.24

Bob then sold the 4 books from the garage sale to his friends for $2.56 each. Bob now had $10.24. "I see double digits!" Bob screamed.

Bob broke into a little dance known as "The RoboCop." He was popping his arms and stepping side to side, singing, "I see double digits, double digits, yeah!"

He had doubled his money. He called Uncle Doubler to update him on the continued progress. After his call, Bod had a new idea on how to double his money. It was time to tweak the business model, just a little. That evening, he accompanied his mom on her weekly grocery shopping trip. Bob bought a case of 24 bottles of water for a total price of $10.24 from the superstore. There was a neighborhood baseball game coming up soon, and Bob was ready to take it to the next level.

Day 11

HOW BOB TURNED $10.24 INTO $20.48

The dog days of summer were upon the sleepy railroad town of Dollarville. On this day, everyone in the neighborhood was gathered for another rousing game of kickball. Kids were having a blast, but Bob insisted on selling instead. For him, there would be no hide-and-seek unless it involved seeking money. He was willing to count to twenty if the price was right.

The day was hot, stuffy, and miserable. Hawking water was exhausting. In his mind, Bob could still hear Ned's maniacal laughter. "Bwahahaha!" The fear of being laughed at sent chills down his spine.

Mom could tell by looking at him he was losing steam. She did not like the sudden drop in enthusiasm.

"I can see you feel so stressed over this." Mom said.

"Being an entrepreneur is not all sunshine and rainbows. It will be long hours and exhausting work," Mom cautioned.

As a cashier, Mom knew a thing or two about being resilient. She was used to the long weekend hours. She also encountered all kinds of

31

people. Sometimes she had to deal with very rude customers. But the job also gave her a chance to meet some very nice people. Just having a conversation with them made her day.

"Do you still want to teach your brothers a lesson?"

Bob looked at her with determination and declared, "Yes, Mom. They need to see me winning. They don't know who I am. I will give them a taste of their own medicine."

"That's my boy! I won't let you fail." Mom was happy. She did not want to see Bob giving up so easily.

Bob bought some peanuts with some of the profit to keep his energy up. He also had to drink some of the water to stay hydrated. He was able to work for the rest of the game.

Bob counted his money. He was selling the water at $1.00 per bottle. A case of 24 bottles of water would have netted him $24.00. But since he drank some of it and bought peanuts with some of the profit, the total was now $20.48.

It turned out that Bob was still able to double his money.

Bob broke into a little dance known as "The Raver." He was waving his arms, jumping up and down, and letting loose. He called Uncle Doubler, who told him, "Bravo, you did a great job!"

That evening, Bob bought 2 comic books for a total of $20.48 at his neighbors' garage sale.

Day 12

HOW BOB TURNED $20.48 INTO $40.96

Ned had a bruised face. He told the parents that he had "walked into a door" at school. Bob knew the story was a fat lie. He knew Ned's unhinged rage too well. He had seen his violent tirades. He had seen him tear doors off their hinges. Ned was always angry, irritable, and unstable. But there was nothing to be gained by questioning it. Bob had a bigger fish to fry. He had money to double.

Bob sold the 2 comic books to his friends for $20.48 each. Bob now had $40.96.

Bob broke into a little dance known as "The Moonwalk." He executed it as smoothly as the King of Pop himself, sliding backward effortlessly on the hardwood floor.

He had doubled his money with yet another product. He called Uncle Doubler. "Congratulations, son! You just keep on going! I am now convinced you are the cash whisperer!" Bob was getting pretty used to the most famous adage about making money: buy low, sell high!

That evening, Bob followed Mom and bought 10 toys for a total of $40.96 at another store that was closing in the neighboring city.

Closing stores usually held a clearance sale. Bob and Mom also learned about an ongoing county fair in the area.

Day 13

HOW BOB TURNED $40.96 INTO $81.92

Bob woke up with the urge to prove the naysayers wrong. He dreamed of the day when he would give them a taste of their own medicine. But that was not his only wish. Bob wished his family lived somewhere else. He longed for a neighborhood with a sense of ease and calm—a place with at least a safe sidewalk. Dollarville had very safe neighborhoods. Maple Avenue was not one of them. Abandoned junk vehicles, debris, tall grass, and weeds occupied what used to be sidewalks.

Most of Dollarville's payday loan joints, dollar stores, bus stops, fast-food restaurants, and liquor stores were on Maple Avenue. But it required advanced urban warfare tactics to navigate. There was always something to dodge if you are not hit by a speeding homicide detective's car. Bob was not allowed to walk alone. With Mom behind for maximum cover, Bob had to avoid rodents and the unusually giant roaches. He had to leap over stinky sewage puddles, litter, and dog waste. He had to steer clear of suspicious plastic bags dancing in the wind and a shady stray dog doing its business. Bob had to duck an empty bottle thrown carelessly out a car window and dozens of cat eyes in the storm drain. You don't walk on Maple Avenue. You survive. There were mean looking pit bulls in the front yards. There were groups of young men hanging around abandoned distressed properties. It was all worth it. Bob was able to sell the toys for a total of $81.92.

For his celebratory dance, Bob started doing "The Sprinkler." Bob pushed his left arm straight out with the right arm bent at the elbow behind his head, moving in and out, bobbing his head up and down.

He had doubled his money. He called Uncle Doubler.

"Excellent!" stated Uncle Doubler. "Recall that all this started with a penny. Your hard work and commitment have paid off."

Bob knew he was lucky to have Uncle Doubler. Mentors can provide you with the information you need to strengthen your business. They can also help you work smarter by steering you clear of the pitfalls.

This experiment was getting interesting, Bob thought. He was more successful than he had thought was possible when he started.

"Well, if I keep doubling my money like this, maybe I can buy Mom a house sooner," Bob thought to himself.

That evening, Bob followed Mom to the neighboring county fair. Bob bought more toys for $81.92. He knew which toys were popular among his friends. This time, he would go over to the neighboring subdivision.

Day 14

HOW BOB TURNED $81.92 INTO $163.84

Mom and Dad had to go to school before work. Both Ned and Nelly had cases in the principal's office. According to the phone call, Ned's charge was physical aggression toward others. Nelly was accused of theft. Bob knew his brothers were probably not innocent. Ned was known to be hostile and rude. It was not the first time he was in trouble for being arrogant, belligerent, or unruly. He thought it was cool to be aggressive. To Ned, everything in life was a battle.

Meanwhile, Nelly carried an "I don't care" attitude like a badge of honor, and he had a knack for taking things that didn't belong to him.

Bob took the time to catch up on his business reality shows. He found them to be both informative and motivating. Bob watched TV with three of his friends from the "Young Entrepreneurs Club" when Nelly came in and started hurling insults. The vibe in the room changed to a hostile one. His insensitive comments made Bob shiver.

Young Entrepreneurs Club was made of kids who were all wildly enthusiastic about finance. All their talk was about money: How to make it, spend it, invest it, multiply it, and share it. They did nothing wrong. Nelly had no reason to treat them the way he did. But this was not out of his character. Nelly had a special hatred for kids who did well in school. He always made sure kids with exceptional academic abilities or ambitious kids like Bob were generally maligned.

"What a bunch of weirdos?"

Bob felt helpless and powerless. He was sad because he could not defend his friends. They were like family to him. They could not understand what is wrong with having academic gifts. They could not pretend to be like everyone else. Luckily for Bob, Nelly was caught by Dad at the end of his long rant. Dad blew his top off. He could not understand why Nelly had to be verbally abusive to Bob and his friends.

"You are about to get on my last nerve." Dad's face contorted in anger. "Chances are you'll end up working for one of these kids."

Nelly was forced to apologize. But his "Sorrrrry" came with a level-10 attitude. It was the most remorseless "sorry" in the history of apologies.

This was also the day that Mom was pushed out of the school PTA because of Ned and Nelly's unbecoming behavior. She came home in a foul mood.

"I am shocked, disgusted, angry," she lamented.

Bob did his best to mind his own business. Selling door to door to neighborhood families was tough. But Bob was tougher. He still made a tidy profit.

Bob sold the toys for $163.84. It was a three-figure milestone. "No way!" Bob was ecstatic about his profit.

Bob broke into a little dance known as "The Pendulum," swinging his arms with glee.

He had doubled his money and finally went past the $100 mark! He called Uncle Doubler.

"Never stop believing. Don't let anyone tell you that you cannot do this," Uncle Doubler encouraged him.

That evening, Bob decided to step up his game. His mom helped him purchase 2 bicycles for a total of $163.84 from a seller they found on local classifieds.

"Wow," Bob thought, still amazed at the fact that this all started with a shiny penny. Bob didn't see his brothers much because he was so busy, and he began to tune them out when they teased him. Bob was just too preoccupied with doubling.

Day 15

HOW BOB TURNED $163.84 INTO $327.68

This was the day when Bob's mean big brother Ned joined Prospect High School. He was older but not wiser. Ned still treated Bob like a little oddity. Although Bob was still in elementary school, he had a few customers at Washington Middle School. Ned always tried to sabotage Bob's business by telling people how inferior his products were. He also enjoyed embarrassing him. On one occasion, Ned had the audacity to tell everyone that Bob's designer label clothes were from a thrift store. It was true, but who does that to his little brother? Bob was not happy.

This day, Bob followed Mom to a swap meet. His mom taught him how to be friendly and courteous to others, make eye contact, and shake hands. The swap meet enabled him to sell to strangers. He learned how to communicate with customers outside his comfort zone.

Bob sold the bicycles for a total of $327.68. He was on a roll!

Bob broke into a little dance known as "The Floss," joyfully alternating swinging his arms around his torso. He was feeling proud of what he had gained.

He had doubled his money yet again! He called Uncle Doubler.

The demand for bicycles was going up, Bob thought. That evening, Bob bought six bicycles with some of the money.

Day 16

HOW BOB TURNED $327.68 INTO $655.36

"Don't walk under that ladder!" a painter shouted. Bob stopped just in time. In Dollarville, walking under a ladder was considered a source of bad luck.

Walking door to door wasn't easy. Bob was on full-blast charm offensive. He had to turn on all his persuasion taps. He narrated about his own experience and told people why owning a bicycle was good for them. In the startup world, "Demo" stands for Demonstration. Demo day is a pitch event where creators showcase their inventions to top investors for a chance at funding. Selling door to door enabled Bob to work on his "Demo" skills. He had to get his point across in 20 seconds or less. His "elevator pitch" was still weak but better than ever before.

Bob was now a student at Washington Middle School on Main Street. It was against the rules to sell items on middle school grounds. Teachers did not want arguments between the sellers and buyers breaking into fights. Bob made sure no rules were broken. The Kids would come with their parents to pick the items, or Bob and Mom would take the item to the kids' place. Eventually, Bob was able to sell all the six bicycles to friends, neighbors, and even strangers!

His total was now $655.36, which included both the profit and the savings.

Not bad. Bob was only in 6th grade, and he was doing better than other 11-year-olds.

Bob broke into a little dance known as "The Dance Flick." He moved so happily because he had now passed the $500 mark.

"Yippeee!" exclaimed Bob.

He had doubled his money. He called Uncle Doubler.

Mom and Dad helped him buy more bicycles at a clearance sale. It was hot, but Bob was determined. He didn't complain, even when they were on their feet for hours, looking through bicycles and choosing the best ones. He was becoming a bargain hunter. He wanted to buy low and sell high—that way, he would make more profit. When he and his parents went home that evening, they ensured the bicycles were ready for sale. His brothers were nowhere in sight because they had started staying later at school for extracurricular activities.

In his sleep, Bob could still hear Ned's maniacal laughter. "Bwahahaha!" It triggered his fear of being ridiculed. The fear of shame and embarrassment was wind in his sails. He felt motivated.

Day 17

HOW BOB TURNED $655.36 INTO $1,310.72

This was an eye-opening day. Dad took Bob to open a savings account at the local bank branch on Main Street. For the first time, Bob deposited some of his money in the bank.

He had a long chat with the personal banker. He learned that when you put money in a savings account or buy bonds, the money earns interest. "The bank pays you interest on deposits you gave them," the personal banker explained.

When the personal banker explained how compound interest works, Bob's jaw dropped in amazement.

"If you leave the original money plus the interest you made in the bank, your interest earns interest, which is known as compound interest."

Bob was fascinated by the magic of the most potent force in the financial universe: compound interest. He told the personal banker to explain the "interest on interest" thing again.

"Let's say you put $100 in a savings account, and each year it earns a 10% return. You earn $10 in interest that year, right? If you leave that $110 in the savings account, it will earn $11 interest the following year. Stay with me. If you leave that $121 in the savings account, well! This keeps going or compounding until you withdraw the funds. The more years, the better, right?"

Bob got the idea. But his mind was still blown!

"Why don't they teach me this in school? Is it illegal?" Bob inquired. He could not believe it. He just found a new way to make his money grow, even while he slept.

"Well, the opposite is also true. Interest is what you pay the bank to borrow its money," the personal banker warned. "See, sometimes you are the lender, and other times you are the borrower."

The personal banker talked about an emergency fund, cash for unexpected expenses. Some people kept their emergency funds in a savings account.

The chat moved on to budgeting.

"A budget is a plan that you make to keep track of your money and where it is going," Dad intervened impatiently. "Let's go, Bob. We are holding the line."

Curious Bob had to be dragged out of the bank.

Dad was proud of Bob. He wanted Bob to be even more successful, so he showed him all the money tricks he knew. He told Bob of a popular type of long-term account for retirement savings that he got through his job at the rail yard. It was known as a 401(k). Bob had heard about it. Many adults talked about 401(k) all the time, so he was very curious about it.

Dad put Bob in charge of developing a budget for family events. That was bound to make his brothers even more bitter and jealous. But they had no interest in listening to what their dad had to say about money and all that jazz. Bob was becoming money wise. He knew how to handle it and was not a big spender.

Bob sold the bicycles he had. His total was now $1,310.72. He had doubled his money and reached the $1,000 mark! He called Uncle Doubler, the one person who listened to him without any agenda of his own.

Back home later that day, Bob broke into a little dance known as "The Hustle," adding his special clap at the end. Dancing helped him keep his mind off the stress.

Bob was holding an imaginary microphone, lip-syncing songs, and dancing when Mom and Dad walked in. They both looked sad and dejected as they slumped on the couch. It turned out that Ned was in the hospital. The story was that he had been beaten up by a group of thugs. Bob was not buying it. He knew it was fishy. It was no secret that Ned was reckless and careless. He was aggressive and arrogant and had an explosive rage. Ned was known to pick fights over nothing. He hated school and was not walking down the right path. Bob knew it. Even Mom and Dad knew the story was fake. Ned was a self-saboteur. He had not been beaten up by a group of thugs. Ned was the thug.

"The part that hurts me the most is the lack of respect," Mom sobbed.

Bob was also still bothered by the discussion he had earlier with the personal banker. He wrote a letter to the principal about investing classes. There was no reason why parents cannot rely on the school system to teach their kids about money, he argued. He also wanted the school to set up an Entrepreneurship Day in Middle school for kids to showcase their business skills. He did not get a response.

As the day was coming to an end, Mom and Dad helped Bob buy more used bikes with the money that was left money. The supply of old bicycles was going down. This time he had to visit three stores to find the bikes at the best prices without compromising quality and style. Bob was the only hope for his family.

Day 18

HOW BOB TURNED $1,310.72 INTO $2,621.44

This was the day when Nelly joined Prospect High School. There was no love lost. Nelly and his friends treated Bob like dirt. They were indifferent to anybody who did well in school. Nelly treated people who loved education or school like a bunch of outcasts. To him, they were traitors. They were out to make him look bad. Nelly also resented people who talked about building businesses. It was as if entrepreneurial curiosity was a highly infectious disease. Bob was tired of Nelly dumping his negative feelings on him. Good riddance, Bob thought. Now, Bob had Washington Middle School all to himself.

Bob worked on the bikes with Dad, who was on vacation. Dad was tough as nails. Track laborer was the most dangerous job in Dollarville. The hazards included working around high-voltage electricity, slippery surfaces, toxic chemicals, and moving trains. Railroad workers performed physically demanding tasks all day. They worked outdoors in all kinds of weather. The work schedule was also crazy. Dad was on call just about every day of the week, 24 hours a day. He was rarely at home. Bob knew Dad was working hard at the yard to keep a roof over their heads and food on the table.

Dollarville Rail Depot was part of the historic Colorado railroad system famous for its national significance. Train engineers loved the picturesque mountain panorama that framed the Mile High City on the west. But that was not the reason all the trains stopped here. The engineers were getting ready to deal with the difficult terrain of the Rocky Mountains. Heading west past Denver City, the railroad passed through some of the nation's most challenging terrain. Dad and his workmates were in charge of the aging transcontinental railroad tracks, maintaining structures and drainage.

Dad believed in hard work and individual responsibility. He taught Bob the importance of earning a decent living. He also taught him good manners, respecting elders, and helping others. Working with Dad was a little frustrating, though. He was not a cheerleader like Mom. He was a Drill Sergeant. He was quick to criticize and slow to praise. It was a pain in the neck to work with a micromanager. Dad would yell at him for something small, which made it less fun for Bob.

Dad's old-school take-no-prisoners approach to work came naturally to him. The wear marks and the stains on his boots told a silent story. Like an ancient record, the boots carried a story of brutal winters, fires and rain, horrors and heroism at the Dollarville rail yard. Like rings on an old tree stump, the stains on his boots were windows in time.

After fixing the bikes, they still needed to find customers and persuade them to buy. Bob began to get anxious about selling the bikes, even though he had done it before. He felt like giving up on his dream. His money journey teetered on the brink of failure. Bob was at the end of his rope. He wasn't sure he could do it anymore, so he had to call Uncle Doubler for some "wisdom nuggets."

"I can't..." he faltered. Uncle Doubler stopped him. He hated self-defeating talk.

"Nonsense, you can do it! Focus on your accomplishments. See how far you have come," Uncle Doubler told him. "Trust me, you got this."

Uncle Doubler never failed to dish out good vibes. He believed that every child has incredible potential. Thanks to him, Bob was able to hang on until all the work was done. He did this by telling himself repeatedly as he worked, "I can do this!"

Bob made sure to take quality naps before heading out to look for new customers. That always made him feel renewed. He was ready for success! He visited another neighborhood and told them about the great benefits of biking. He made good sales that day. His total was now $2,621.44, including the money in his savings account and inventory. Not bad. Bob was only in 7th grade, and he was doing better than other 12-year-olds.

Selling was tough and stress-inducing on a normal day. Working with a demanding boot-camp boss like Dad Bob made it worse. Bob broke into a little dance known as "The Monkey." It felt great to dance and release the pent-up stress.

Bob had doubled his money. He called Uncle Doubler, his mentor. "Truly amazing!"

He deposited some money in his savings account. With the rest, Mom helped him buy more used bikes. They spent hours searching for bargains on auction sites and in classified ads. They combed through the flea market on Sellers Street, Dollarville. They sniffed through garage sales, estate sales, thrift shops, yard sales, and clearance racks at department stores. They traveled far distances for deals.

Mom was a great business mentor and helper. Mom always taught him to be thrifty with money. She bought items only when there was a discount and would haggle to save five cents.

"Buy low, sell high. It's a mantra that has been around for thousands of years," she would say for the umpteenth time. Bob was so grateful for his parents.

Day 19

HOW BOB TURNED $2,621.44 INTO $5,242.88

It was a scene straight out of a movie set. The presence of the Dollarville Police Department at the school caused a major alarm and disruption. Nelly was briefly detained and later released for creating a hit list. The rules that prohibited bullying, harassment, and making hit lists were clearly posted on the walls. The hit list entitled "Teacher's pets" was turned in to a teacher by a fellow student. It contained names of those he wanted to harm. Kids with exceptional academic abilities were still his primary target. The kids who were usually smartly dressed were also on the list. Nelly's goal was to make the kids feel insecure and embarrassed about their achievements. Mom had to plead with the principal to let Nelly stay in school. He wanted him gone for good. She argued that the list was just teenage banter.

The drama did not end at school. The home was a hostile environment on this day. Nelly would only speak in monosyllabic grunts or shrugs. Like a baby tasting his first lemon, Nelly's face remained screwed up. His bitterness and resentment were products of the desire to blame others. It was never his fault. He would not even say hello to family members. Bob found him strangely distant for a brother. Ned was worse. He remains stone-faced most of the day. He was a time bomb. He was always throwing objects, kicking doors, or punching walls when Dad was not home. He was in trouble in school for constantly getting into fights with other high school seniors. Almost every time a physical altercation broke out, Ned was involved. Living with Ned and Nelly was like living in a war zone.

Bob could not understand why gifted students should be bullied just for having exceptional school performance. It did not make sense. But business activities gave Bob an excuse to dodge any interactions with his mean brothers. He worked on the bicycles, this time with Uncle Noah. He was the best with this kind of project. Uncle Noah was mechanically inclined and handy. He also knew many bicycle and motor mechanics. They now had a stand at a local swap shop. This meant that Bob had to work a little longer and harder. Even when the bikes were ready, he still had to do a tremendous amount of work to persuade customers to part with their money. The school was also getting harder for him, and sometimes he found himself nodding off in class.

"Remember the deal you made with your dad to keep your grades up," Uncle Noah cautioned.

Bob had also promised himself to keep his grades up. Though he was young, he knew that business alone wouldn't make him successful. He knew that education led to better job opportunities and better quality of life. School also provided a market for him. He had a network of classmates who doubled as his customers and his ambassadors.

In Dollarville, Barber shops were more popular than the Mayor's office. Bob knew that this where people came together to catch up on the latest gossip and news. He sang and danced his way into the hearts of everyone in the local barbershops. He was known as the cute dancing kid.

It was worth the effort. He sold many bicycles. Bob added up all his assets: cash at hand, the money in the bank, and the remaining bicycles. The other name for unsold items is inventory. Bob had a total of $5,242.88 in assets. Not bad. Bob was only in 8th grade, and he was doing better than other 13-year-olds.

Bob did not forget to celebrate the success. He broke into a little dance known as "The Dougie" and sang, "Teach me how to double. Hey, Uncle taught me how to double, yaaayyyyy."

He had doubled his money. He called Uncle Doubler, his consultant. Uncle Doubler was happy to hear the news. He knew the importance of gaining a positive market response.

He deposited some money into his interest-bearing savings account. With the remainder, he added more bicycles for their shop stand.

"What a day, what a day!" Bob thought.

Day 20

HOW BOB TURNED $5,242.88 INTO $10,485.76

The ringtone on Mom's phone was unmistakable. Her face revealed anger and disappointment. It was the principal's office. Bob's parents needed to go to school at day's end for a meeting. Bob thought Nelly had antagonized his teachers again. It turned out he had skipped school on senior skip day. First of all, Nelly wasn't a senior. Secondly, senior skip day was against school rules.

Ned was not doing well either. He was now out of high school. He refused to go to college or trade school, and he turned down an offer to work with Dad at the rail yard.

Bob was now a student at Prospect High School on Main Street in Dollarville. It took a while to get acquainted with the high school culture. He wanted to know if "freshman" bullying real or it was just a myth. Then he quickly realized that his own brothers were the bullies. Whenever the topic was raised, it was all about the Benjamins brothers. Ned and Nelly treated people who loved school, science, or business like a bunch of outcasts. For them, success in education was not cool. Ned was of the most popular instigators in the history of Prospect High School. Reportedly, whenever a scuffle broke out, and chairs came out flying, Ned was not far. The teachers were happy to see a good Benjamin in Bob. They could not believe he was related to Ned and Nelly.

Like many high school students around the world, Bob took daily lessons in history, math, biology, chemistry, and other subjects. For some unknown reason, the teachers never touched the financial terms that Uncle Doubler threw around. There were campaigns to get kids interested in science, technology, engineering, and math fields but not entrepreneurship. There should be a day for students to showcase startup ideas and business concepts. Bob sent an urgent letter to the principal of Prospect High School. He wanted to know why school kids were kept in the dark about things like assets, bonds, budget, cash flow, compound interest, credit, credit score, debt, demand, diversification, dividend, earning, emergency fund, entrepreneurship, expenses, generational wealth, giving, identity theft, income, insurance, interest, inventory, investing, liabilities, loan, loss, mutual funds, need vs. wants, net worth, opportunity cost, profit, real estate, risk, savings, setting money goals, spending, stocks, supply, taxes, trade-offs, and even 401(k). Was it a government secret? He received no response. Not a word. Just... crickets.

Prospect High School was an excellent place to get customers. But it was also against the rules to sell items on high school grounds.

Teachers knew students might start selling unhealthy and illegal items. They did not want high school students to be high on their own supplies. Bob did not have to break any rules to do business. His old cash and delivery system was still working. He made sure the students knew he had the best bicycles on the planet. There's nothing quite like word of mouth when it comes to promoting a product in high school.

A good entrepreneur is never satisfied with the status quo. Tweaking and testing business ideas were always on top of Bob's mind. It was time to elevate his game.

This day he was looking into ways to produce multiple streams of income. He started making money doing side hustles like raking leaves and mowing lawns. He was into dog walking and pet sitting. He offered car washing and detailing services. It required a lot of time and patience to pull this off.

Bob also frequented the local library to learn about words that were being thrown around by adults. It was an eye-opening experience. In the process he learned how to better manage personal finances and improve credit scores. It was as if the books were written by his mentor. Making money was one thing, but keeping it was equally important. He could almost hear Uncle Doubler screaming in the books, "Go out there, son. Stay out of debt. Buy low! Sell high! Earn! Save! Invest! Repeat!"

The part about identity theft scared him most. This is when someone takes your personal information without your permission in order to commit a crime. The thief can open credit card accounts in your name or sell your information. Many hackers want to breach computer systems to steal personal information. This could cause you serious problems later.

"Scammers want to be part of your life," one book warned.

Bob also learned about wants versus needs. It now made sense why his mom would clip coupons and do comparison shopping. Mom was always smart shopping!

Bob sold the rest of the bicycles at the swap shop. His total was now $10,485.76 from the side jobs and the bicycles. Not bad. Bob was only 14 years old. He was doing better than other high school freshmen.

He was excited when he got home that evening. Bob broke into a little dance known as "The Lawnmower," acting as if he was mowing the lawn. He had so much fun! He rarely saw his brothers. It was probably better that way, he thought.

He had doubled his money. He called Uncle Doubler, the wise and trusted counselor. Uncle Doubler was pleased to hear about Bob's multiple streams of income strategy. He knew the importance of achieving and maintaining a positive cash flow.

Uncle Noah then helped Bob buy two used trucks with some of the money.

This was a huge step. Bob was excited and nervous at the same time. Uncle Noah was great at selecting cars. He knew which cars sold well in Dollarville, the easiest vehicles to flip, and where to find them. He taught Bob how to inspect and evaluate a potential flip. Bod needed to learn how to spot and avoid lemons. These were defective vehicles that were too damaged for repair.

Day 21

HOW BOB TURNED $10,485.76 INTO $20,971.52

Bob was woken up by Mom screaming on the phone, again. She had just learned that Ned was now a guest in county jail. He was facing, at a minimum, a one-year license suspension and three years of probation. Mom and Dad were tired of continually bailing out Ned. "Stop! Enough!" Mom was wearing the saddest face Bob had ever seen.

Bob was worried about his brothers. They did not see eye-to-eye, but they were still family.

Bob worked on the trucks with Dad and Uncle Noah over the summer. He spent his spare time learning how to successfully buy, fix, and sell old cars. It was difficult. It took passion, hard work, and resilience. With school, it was a challenge, but Bob was committed. Some of the work had to be done by skilled professionals like motor mechanics and auto body repair technicians.

Slowly but surely, the trucks and the side jobs brought in big bucks. His total was now $20,971.52. Not bad. Bob was only 15 years old, and he was doing better than other high school sophomores.

Bob broke into a little dance known as "The Hammer," singing, "Bang bang, I'm a kid with a plan. Bang bang, I'll be rich before I'm a man." He laughed at his rhyming lyrics.

He had doubled his money again. He called Uncle Doubler, his special confidant. "Way to go!"

With that money, Uncle Noah helped Bob buy more used cars. This was a whole different ball game, but Bob was ready after all he had learned from the business, school, and life so far. He was ready and even excited.

Bob now knew his way around the dealer auctions and how to find great deals. He chose the best cars at the best prices.

Day 22

HOW BOB TURNED $20,971.52 INTO $41,943.04

The sound of military boots on the pavement outside punctured the morning quiet. It was followed by Mom and Dad running for the door. Ned and Nelly had been missing for a while. Mom had spent many sleepless nights worrying about where Ned and Nelly were, who they were with, and what they were doing. No mother wants to see her kids falling off the social ladder. Both were bizarre and unpredictable.

The sheriff had some news. Nelly had been found west of Silver Run Park, loudly arguing with some trees. He had either consumed something bad or he was emotionally at rock bottom. Probably both. Nelly was now out of high school. Bob was surprised that the principal did not send a card to say good riddance to the worst student in the history of Prospect High School. He had given the teachers a hard time. If Nelly was not ignoring instructions, he was using a disrespectful tone of voice. He failed most of the subjects. He forgot that bad attitudes don't get positive results. Nelly did not go to college or trade school after high school. Like Ned, he refused to work with Dad at the rail yard. Mom and Dad quickly followed the sheriff to the streets.

Bob continued working on the cars and selling them. He missed many high school football games and other fun activities. When other kids had rap battles, Bob had sale demos. Bob was totally cool with delayed   gratification. What would Uncle Doubler say? "Everything in life has an opportunity cost!"

Some students made fun of his business ventures, but Mom had a good answer for this. "You don't have to try to be normal, or as other people, you're already extraordinary in my books."

Bob learned to shrug it off and keep going. He focused hard on both academics and entrepreneurship. The mean students' muffled laughter did not bother him anymore. Bob was sick of being paraded around like a little oddity.

 The car flipping and the side jobs paid off big time. The trade-off was worthwhile. His net worth was now $41,943.04. Net worth is what you own minus what you owe. Not bad. Bob was only 16, and he was doing better than other high school juniors.

Sometimes, Bob reflected upon his journey so far. He couldn't believe this all started with a dream and a coin. A big, fat bank account was not required. He pinched himself a couple of times, just to ensure this was real. "Ouch!" It was. It was really real.

Bob broke into a little dance known as "The Hokey Pokey" while shouting, "Hokey pokey yaaayyyy!"

He had doubled his money, and his total was becoming even more impressive. He called Uncle Doubler, his guru. "You're in the big leagues now, son," he laughed.

With that money, Bob bought more used cars. He realized he enjoyed going to the shops to observe, try out, and choose the best ones. It gave him a thrill.

It was a good day. But on the other hand, Ned was still missing. He was still on his three-year probation, and his driving license was still suspended. Bob's relationship with both his brothers remained contentious, but he still wished them well. Ned did not deserve an awful life. The family was worried.

Day 23

HOW BOB TURNED $41,943.04 INTO $83,886.08

The phone rang incredibly early in the morning. Ned had just been spotted sleeping under the bridge on the outskirts of Dollarville. Apparently, life had thrown him into a highly distressed mental state. He was alone, broke, unemployable, and clearly losing his sanity. The bridge was on one of America's most haunted roads and was located on what was known as "Mystery Mile." No human went to that part of town after dusk, let alone sleeping. The enclave under the bridge also had a name: "Dead man's cave." Ned's driving license was no longer suspended. But he was still on his three-year probation. If he was caught doing stuff, he would do some time in jail. He was reportedly fine. The family was happy to hear he was still alive. Nelly was not doing well either. He was currently living in the abandoned murder mystery motel on State Highway 79.

Dad decided to spend his remaining free time helping Bob. Bob worked on the cars with Dad and Uncle Noah. It was hard work. When he was not inspecting a car's engine oil, radiator, belts, transmission, brakes, and vehicle identification number (VIN), Bob was negotiating prices, bidding, or selling. He sold most of the cars by advertising in the local newspaper and on social media.

He also continued to work on the side jobs. He had added selling used books, T-shirts, and sneakers to the list. Additionally, there were exams and papers to turn in, and he had to get ready for high school graduation.

He had to miss some of the parties because he spent his nights reading and researching ways to make the business better. He had to learn business etiquette and how to handle high-stress environments.

Sometimes he struggled to make sales. He was disappointed with himself. In his mind he could hear Nelly laughing mischievously and making the "cuckoo" sign to Ned. It was a sad memory. He was on the brink of quitting multiple times and had to call his mentor for some wisdom nuggets. "Mistakes don't mean you should stop. Failures are part of the process. Keep going!" Uncle Doubler would advise.

Bob was relieved when Day 23 finally came. His total was now $83,886.08. Not bad. Bob was only 17 years. He was doing way better than the other high school seniors.

It was time to get popping. He had to do a scary celebratory dance move this time. "The Thriller!" This was getting real. "Cause this is a thriller, thriller night," he did some cool moves to the sound of MJ.

Bob had doubled his money despite the difficulties. He called Uncle Doubler, his trusted cheerleader.

It was time to kick it up a notch.

With the money, Aunt Sophia helped get into real estate investments. They started looking for his first condo to flip! House flipping is when you buy a cheap house, fix it up, and resell it for profit. She loved teaching first-time flippers the tricks of the trade. For her nephew, she was ready to go the extra mile. Aunt Sophia had great knowledge of the real estate market. She introduced Bob to the industry players like realtors, electricians, carpenters, joiners, plumbers, brick layers, landscapers, terminators, and waste haulers. Finding a deal was difficult. It took a lot of time and research. Many times, he lost a deal to competitors. He was not the only shark in the ocean.

Aunt Sophia was a great motivator and nice to work with. "You need to make baby steps into real estate investing. And don't worry. Failure, for entrepreneurs, is inevitable," she would say.

Aunt Sophia was a therapist, not a Drill Sergeant like Dad. She was the cool aunt who listened without being judgmental. Even in the most challenging times, she was one of his greatest cheerleaders. She was known for reciting the real estate mantra "location, location, location." Aunt Sophia was always armed with a bursting tool belt, and she wasn't afraid to use it on short notice. She knew how to turn an ugly house into a dramatic dream home.

They found a condo at Lincoln Street that was in foreclosure. A foreclosure is what happens when a homeowner fails to pay the loan on the house, and the bank takes possession of it. The house becomes a bank-owned property. The bank then sells it usually for a low price. Bob bought it at an auction for $60,000. Aunt Sophia thought it was a good deal.

"That was a steal!"

Day 24

HOW BOB TURNED $83,886.08 INTO $167,772.16

Bob was having a perfectly good morning. Bob was now a student at Silverton University off Bull Run Highway. He was studying interior design with a minor in economics. Bob was the first in the family to attend college. It was a huge milestone. He was glad that the days when he lived in constant fear of being bullied were over.

This started like an innocent day, but it wasn't. Mom was already at his door, with a little request. She wanted Bob to give his brothers a chance at his business. Bob's stomach twisted in knots as he paused to think for a minute, staring blankly out the window. The request triggered a rush of anger, fear, and pain. It made his blood boil. In his mind, Bob could still hear Nelly laughing mischievously and gesturing a cuckoo sign to Ned when they were young. He could even hear an echo of Ned's maniacal laughter in response. Bob was surprised they dared to send Mom to him seeking help.

"They are in a bad situation," she pleaded. "They don't know what to do."

Bob had a lot of respect for Mom. Mom was always a good advocate for all her kids. She was also a fighter. Bob had watched his family struggle to pay bills. They lived in a predominantly working-class neighborhood where many families were living hand to mouth.

Ned and Nelly were struggling to make ends meet. They were both grown-up men now. Nelly was 20. Ned was 22 years old.

They did odd jobs to get some money but did not make enough money to support themselves. Mom continued to support them financially as if they were young kids. They both desperately needed ways to get a good income.

Nelly was in debt up to his eyeballs. He could not make his credit card payments on time. His credit history was bad, and his credit score was very low. He could not get a good job or an apartment anywhere on the planet.

Ned was also a financial train wreck. He was in debt and had no savings at all. His credit history was bad. He always wanted expensive things to impress his friends. He bought trendy clothes and shoes with credit cards. He bought fast food and costly coffee with borrowed money. He spent even more on smartphones, apps, and travel.

Ned was already in trouble for writing checks without enough funds in his account. The checks bounced like basketballs. A bounced check occurs when the writer of the check has insufficient funds in the account. Passing bad checks can be illegal. It's a serious crime. It can also lead to bank fees, penalties, and a bad credit score. Considering that Ned had just completed three-year probation, things were getting out of hand. He was dancing with the devil. Although Mom was deeply upset by their irresponsible behavior, she was still determined to find solid employment.

Bob was still blankly staring out the window. His eyes were on the snow-covered Rocky Mountains. But his mind was a million miles away.

Mom felt like she was talking to a brick wall, but she did it anyway. "I guess youthful independence and rebellion did not work out. Let them see you winning," She persuaded him.

Bob discovered lingering hard feelings that he was not aware of. He remembered how the brothers had become intolerant of his quest for excellence, putting him down at every opportunity. The way they were mocking his money making projects and talking badly about him to his schoolmates. And now they want a piece of this? No!

Bob loved his brothers, but it would be draining to be near them. The two would test his limits and boundaries the same way they did with teachers, parents, and even police. He had to protect his little positive space. He could not for a minute imagine dealing with Nelly's constant complaining, whining, and pouting. The nasty words, back talk, sarcasm, and callousness would suck the life out of him. He could not bring himself to see Ned as an employee given his aggressive, arrogant, belligerent, and unruly behavior and his explosive rage. Ned would pick fights over nothing. Bob was not ready to face internal resistance. Who would hire people he already knew to be hostile and rude?

Mom was still talking to a statue. Bob was busy trying to fight the anger that was slowly building up through his body. His body was filling up quick with a dangerous mixture of wrath, fury, and explosive rage. He could not let Mom see it.

"My son, forgiveness is the enemy of bad attitudes. The greatest revenge is massive success. Don't dwell on the past. A new chapter doesn't begin unless an old chapter ends."

Then Mom started blaming her own parenting skills. "It was all my fault, but there is nothing you can do to change the past."

That shook Bob to life. He never wanted to hear Mom condemn herself. She had done the best she could. She was not a bad parent just because his brothers messed up. This was one of the most difficult conundrums Bob had ever faced in his life. He did not want to make the already strained relationship worse.

Mom's mental health added to the dilemma. She was often held emotionally hostage. Nelly was a talented manipulator. He played the victim card like a chess champion. He knew which buttons to press when Mom wouldn't "lend" him money. "Nice knowing you. Let me end up on the streets and die" was Nelly's favorite line. It always did the trick. Nelly knew that no parent ever wants to imagine their child starving to death on the sidewalk.

It hurt Bob to see his mom so drained. Although Bob had conflicted feelings towards Mom's idea, he always treated her opinions with reverence, awe, and respect. She always made him feel energized, inspired, happy and optimistic. He was not sure if the arrangement will work even for a day. He regarded his brothers with wariness. They made him feel exhausted, depressed, annoyed, and anxious. But the last thing he wanted was to let Mom down, so he caved.

Mom organized a quick meeting and obligated Ned and Nelly to be on their best behavior. Bob accepted his brothers' apologies, and the three brothers agreed to make peace...

"No matter what, we're brothers for life," Bob reassured, followed by a cheeky, "But never forget I told you I would double the money."

"Well, we were not listening, were we?" Ned joked.

"Apparently not."` Bob's replied, his voice dripping with vindication.

"Yes, bro, and we're glad you didn't listen to us too, or you wouldn't be doing this now," Nelly chimed in to rescue his big brother. "We were blind, but now we see, bro. Now we see," he added as they all hugged.

Bob tabled his conditions. Ned had to complete an anger management program to start working for Bob. Nelly had to undergo substance abuse treatment. Bob laid down the law. The boundaries Bob set were not up for debate. He let them know that there would be consequences for their actions. He was not just the little brother but their new boss. Ned and Nelly promised to work hard.

In the house flipping business, "Demo" stands for "Demolition." Demo day is the sledge-hammer-swinging event when the crew starts tearing down parts of a building for renovation.

This demo day started with great excitement. The sledgehammers started swinging as if to vent out the awkwardness of the moment. Ned felt like a kid in a candy store. Bob and Nelly had to stand back as Ned released pent-up anger on the walls and kitchen counters. It was the first time in his life anyone let him break things without judgment or consequences. No one was telling him to calm down. No one was threatening to sic the police on him. He was even being paid to destroy things. Ned mercilessly hammered the old TVs, ceramic pots, plates, and cups. With each whack, Ned felt stress and anxiety slowly leaving his body. He had just discovered a new way to relax and de-stress better than the anger management program. He yelled and shouted like a maniac. With each smash, his smile grew bigger. Then it happened. Ned flashed the warmest smile Bob had ever seen.

Bob worked on the condo with his brother Nelly over the summer. House flipping was not as easy as it looked on TV, where they show happy people picking out the finishes, light fixtures, paint color, countertops, and tile. He had to hire carpenters, plumbers, and electricians. He had to do a lot of manual work to save money and make a profit. It was blood, sweat, and tears! The fear of making a loss made him shiver.

Bob had to prepare a profit-and-loss statement and other financial statements. He was glad for the days he had spent in the library learning about that stuff. He still had to hire an accountant for some of the work, though. Developing detailed budgets was not fun. He had to deal with selling costs, insurance, and property taxes. The stress of marketing the property and dealing with lowball offers was also extremely frustrating.

He knew that the rigors of entrepreneurship demanded blood and sweat sacrifices. But he didn't know how much. Bob was tired. There was a little voice in his head saying, "There is no future in this"

"Urgh! Why did I even think it was a good idea?" Bob lamented. It was not as glamorous as it looked on TV.

He had to call Uncle Doubler for some wisdom nuggets. Uncle Doubler was pleased to hear that Bob was now in the real estate business. He knew the importance of implementing a scalable marketing strategy. He coached him on how to deal with the current situation. He taught him how to budget and comparison shop for building materials. "Extra, unexpected repairs could cost thousands of dollars," Uncle Doubler cautioned.

He warned him about cash flow, the net amount of cash being transferred into and out of a business. "You have to watch your cash flow. Always remember, income is money coming in. Expenses mean the money going out. Profit is the money left once expenses are paid," Uncle Doubler emphasized.

Uncle Doubler was an excellent motivator. He always managed to get Bob fired up!

"Be the best version of yourself every day," he told Bob. "Most importantly, no matter how bad things get, you should never give up!"

Luckily, the housing market was not so bad. The demand was still high and supply low. Bob was able to sell the condo for a good chunk of money.

Day 24 had finally come. His total was now $167,772.16. Not bad. Bob was only 18 years old. He was doing better than other college freshmen.

Bob and Nelly broke into a little dance known as "The Hully Gully." Dancing helped Bob empty his body of the lingering pent-up anger and resentment toward his brothers.

After a lot of hard work, he had doubled his money again. He called Uncle Doubler, his always-approachable adviser.

While Bob focused on his businesses, studies, and academic learning, he did not forget efforts to promote young entrepreneurship in Dollarville. He hoped that current and future students will have opportunities like he had. Bob tried to pitch the idea to Silverton University. He did not get a response. It was dead on arrival.

"Is it not the entrepreneurs who create the jobs in this country?" he argued. His reasonable begging was to no avail. There was no response.

With some of the money, he bought more bank-owned houses at a city auction. The properties were on Lien Avenue. But buyers were not allowed to look inside before the auction. Bob did not know the condition of the houses. It was another risky move. But it was time to raise the stakes. Bob knew that to achieve his goal, he needed to be firing on all cylinders.

Day 25

HOW BOB TURNED $167,772.16 INTO $335,544.32

Mom was known as the coupon queen on Main Street in Dollarville. But she considered herself an authority on comparison shopping. She would always compare the different prices at which a product was sold before buying that product. She did the same with services. Dad was also a very smart consumer. He never missed a chance to negotiate for a better price; after all, he worked hard for his dollars. He would always haggle, especially when purchasing an expensive item. He was never afraid to ask for a discount.

Mom and Dad spent their adult lives preaching against impulse buying. They had their own wisdom nuggets to dish, such as, "A fool and his money are soon parted," and "A penny saved is a penny earned."

Mom was happy that Bob was giving his brothers a chance to earn a living. On this day, she requested Bob help his brothers create personal budgets. She wanted them to start radically trimming expenses and paying off all debts.

Earning was not enough. She wanted both Ned and Nelly to stop living beyond their means, and she was still worried about their overspending and poor purchase decisions. She complained about how they needed to differentiate between needs and wants at their age. They were embarrassing the coupon queen of Dollarville. Bob promised Mom he would give it his all.

The houses at Lien Avenue turned out to be total wrecks. One house had layers of dust, dangerous mold, and cockroach poop all over. Bob uncovered many safety issues and code violations behind the walls. It was a home for snakes, mice, spiders, bed bugs, roaches, and maggots. The porch rails were missing. Weeds and overgrown shrubs filled the lawn. Someone had to clean it out. It was time to see how the rookies performed under pressure, Bob reasoned. His better angels told him the bullying happened when they were all kids, but the little devil in him begged to differ. There is no statute of limitations in the karmic justice system. There is no sealing of juvenile records in poetic justice law.

"You two start with the gray one," Bob commanded, pointing at the invested property. It was a test. Ned and Nelly obeyed without a murmur. They toiled on the house for hours.

Watching negative Ned and naysayer Nelly wrestle with creepy bugs in a cloud of cockroach poop, mold, and dust was something money couldn't buy. Given the way they had treated his projects in the past, this was poetic justice. The time had come for them to take their medicine. For a moment, Bob was conflicted.

"You missed a spot," Bob joked to mask the feeling of guilt. Bob did not want to think of it as retribution. He was, after all, a forgiving person.

"I know we made mistakes, but please don't rub it in," Nelly pleaded. He had sensed the unwarranted aggression.

Bob was now the big boss. Being the big boss was often boring, lonely, and challenging. Working with family members was awkward at first. He had to set boundaries and make deals. It was the brothers' turn to complain to Mom about their boss Bob. His brothers still got on his nerves, but he tried not to lash out. He wanted the new arrangement to work.

It also turned out that Ned and Nelly were both mechanically inclined. Nelly could intuitively see how things work quickly. Ned was good with tools and machinery.

Renovating the houses was very draining. Bob was covered in dust and sweat for days. He fell and almost lost a tooth. At some point, Bob had paint fall on his face. He had sewer, foundation, roof, and drainage issues in nearly every property. He spent more time and money on these projects than he had planned to. Bob's joy quickly turned to disappointment. He was at his wits' end.

He called Uncle Doubler. "Buy a rundown house, fix it up, and then sell it for a big profit!" he screamed. "They lied, Uncle!"

"But you wanted to do this," Uncle Doubler reminded him. "They don't call it sweat equity for nothing, son."

Uncle Doubler advised him to take a brief time out. Bob took a mental health walk. Then he danced his brains out. He loved the energy that music provided. Dance movement therapy helped him decompress. He returned to work refreshed.

When Day 25 arrived, Bob's profit was worth the waiting. His net total was now $335,544.32. Not bad. Bob was only 19 years old. He was doing better than other college sophomores.

Bob called a team meeting. They broke into a little dance known as "The Electric Slide." They moved their feet left, right, then they went low, and then high! He brought it around and did it all over again.

He had doubled his money. He called his always-available coach.

"Go, Bob!" Uncle Doubler exclaimed. He was so happy for his nephew's success. "This is how we create generational wealth, son."

Uncle Doubler never failed to boost his confidence and self-image. Bob believed him and kept the phrase "generational wealth" in his head.

Main Street appeared to be trapped in time, life standing still. Nothing much had changed for a long time. Bob used some of the money to buy the iconic building on Main Street and Gold Bar Road, a block away from the City Hall. It was his first commercial building. It was a big deal. He had to take out a mortgage for this one. A mortgage is a type of loan you can use to buy a house or a building. Bob had no problem getting pre-approved for a mortgage because he had proof of income, a down payment, and excellent credit.

Bob thought it was an excellent time to pitch his youth economic empowerment idea to City Hall. Bob hand-delivered a letter to the mayor's office asking the city to establish a day for Dollarville City to promote youth entrepreneurship. He argued that Dollarville needed to design a program that would provide financial education and other support to upcoming entrepreneurs. He did not hear back.

That night, Bob remembered he had schoolwork to complete, so he got to that because he was adamant about not giving up on school. It was his father's dream. Bob was not perfect by any means. He had his dark days. He was constantly fighting his inner demons too. Every day, he went to battle with distractions, fatigue, and negativity. He had to fight self-doubt and negative thinking patterns. His personal struggle with procrastination was particularly frustrating. The college workload was backbreaking. But the million dollar question was: how was he going to get to Day 30 when he barely made it through day 27?

Day 26

HOW BOB TURNED $335,544.32 INTO $671,088.64

Bob spent part of the morning drooling over properties on John Street. It was difficult to walk along John Street without being taken aback by the beauty. It was known for its stunning views and tree branches drooping over the streets. The huge single-family houses. The family-friendly backyards. John Street was home to the most expensive pieces of real estate in Dollarville. Most homes were close to the beautiful parks. Bob liked the laid-back yet elegant vibe of the neighborhood.

It felt like a different planet. Everything was different, from the finely manicured landscaping to trendy restaurants and yoga studios. There were no back-to-back payday loan joints, fast-food restaurants, and liquor stores nearby. There were no stinky sewage puddles. As far as his eyes could see, there were no abandoned junk vehicles, boarded properties, or debris. Just kids playing on granite sidewalks, people jogging and walking their dogs. The air was cleaner. He had one special person in mind. The words from Mom were still fresh.

"Don't forget your mama when you become rich and famous."

But first, he had to double his money. It was time for masks, goggles, sledgehammers, and crowbars! Bob knew this was going to be a do or die kind of a day. He worked on the Main Street building with his brothers and Aunt Sophia. The building was old. It was dusty, dirty, and a little smelly. He did not like what he saw. He had his work cut out for him: the peeling exterior paint, the dead lawn, the broken windows, the weathered roof, the mold, the rats. The project turned out to be much more difficult than he had expected when he started.

Cough! Cough! Cough!

"I can't believe I bought this property! Ugh! Yikes! Tear the place down!" Bob thought.

Bob had doubts about this place, but he learned not to say these things too loudly. He had to do his best and see how things unfolded. Now he knew that behind every success, there's struggle, stress, and even fear.

Bob missed a lot of college parties. He chose to spend his time chasing his dream instead of going to parties. Uncle Doubler thought it was a worthwhile trade-off.

"Everything in life has an opportunity cost," Uncle Doubler would say. "By deferring some instant gratification today, you can enjoy greater luxuries later."

It took Bob a while to find a buyer. Few saw the building's value and vision until one day… he finally sold the building! His new total was $671,088.64. Not bad. Bob was only 20 years old. He was doing better than many adults of his age.

The crew broke into a little dance known as "Tootsie Roll." "To the left! To the left! To the right! To the right!"

He had doubled his money with yet another venture. He called Uncle Doubler, the one person who saw the entrepreneurship potential in him he hadn't yet seen in himself.

"Wow, you passed the 500K mark, kid. That's quite an accomplishment."

It was time to pick up the pace. With the money, Bob acquired 5 more houses. This was one of those deals that were high-risk, high reward. The auctions were held on the courthouse steps. Bob was now unstoppable. The sweet smell of victory was in the air.

Day 27

HOW BOB TURNED $671,088.64 INTO $1,342,177.28

Bob could not stop thinking about the John Street homes. The thought of a two-car garage gave him sleepless nights. He imagined the enormous kitchen that his mom spent her life dreaming about and the astonishment as he hands her the keys to a new house. He could picture Mom relaxing on the covered front porch and enjoying her spacious new yard.

Bob continued working on stinky houses with his brothers and Aunt Sophia. Budgeting for the renovation was not as simple as he thought it would be. The ugly houses needed extreme makeovers. They had discolored and sagging gray sidings. Transforming them into beautiful homes would not be easy. Bob had to create a detailed plan that included renovation costs. Making mistakes would lead to a significant loss.

Meanwhile, there were exams and papers to turn in because he had to get ready for college graduation. He had to skip some parties, but it was all worthwhile.

He sold the houses for a good profit. His total was now $1,342,177.28. Not bad. That was a tidy sum of money. The million-dollar mark. The coveted seven figures! Bob's parents had never reached this level of doubling money. Most people in the world would probably never reach this milestone. At 21, Bob was doing better than many adults of any age.

The crew broke into a little dance known as "YMCA," where they used their hands to make the letters Y, M, C, and A. It filled their small office with joy.

He had doubled his money. He called Uncle Doubler, the special person in his life who had seen something in him he hadn't seen himself.

"Yes, my nephew, you diiiiid it! Nothing can stop you now as long as you remain focused, diligent, and creative." With the million mark already in the pocket, Bob thought it was safe to up the ante.

By now, Bob knew how to look through contracts with a fine-tooth comb and smell a deal from 10 miles away. He used some of the money to buy a bigger commercial building. The buying process was much more complicated than previous investments. Bob had to network with brokers, bankers, leasing agents, realtors, and attorneys. But he was ready for whatever came his way.

His mother's dream home propelled him to work even harder.

Day 28

HOW BOB TURNED $1,342,177.28 INTO $2,684,354.56

This was the day when Bob secretly attended an open house on John Street. Bob never forgot his roots, and his mom had always taught him to find something good to do with his money. She taught him to be humble, kind and warned him about selfishness and greed. It was Bob's lifelong dream to buy Mom a house with an enormous kitchen. Bob recalled how his journey had started.

"Keep it, Bob," his mom had said. "You picked it up, so you'll have all the good luck." Don't forget your mama when you become rich and famous!"

He had an action plan in place for Mom's gift. He found nice houses, but he was not ready to tell anyone in the family. The secret was ringing in his ears loudly enough to prompt a click! His brain was his biggest enemy.

Bob worked on the building with his brothers and Aunt Sophia again. The stakes were much higher when flipping a commercial building. Every tenant wanted their office designed a certain way.

The renovations took longer and cost him more money than he had planned. He also incurred many other costs like taxes, marketing, and realtor commissions. Bob discovered that selling commercial properties was not as quick as selling houses.

At one point, Bob had to borrow extra cash from the bank to complete the repairs. The bank ran his credit history. Luckily, Bob still had a great credit score, so he could borrow some money from the bank.

It did not take long to find customers after renovation. He was able to sell the building for profit. His total was now more than $2,684,354.56.

Bob, Nelly, Ned, and Aunt Sophia broke into a little dance known as "Macarena," moving their hands to the beat, then doing a little twist at the end and saying, "Heyyy Macarena, ayyyeee!"

He had successfully doubled his money again. He called Uncle Doubler the one person who believed in him whenever he faltered.

"Bob, I'm proud of you. Keep at it!"

With some of the money, he bought two office buildings. He was almost at the finish line. Thinking of the future Mom's home served as a "drip" of motivation.

Day 29

HOW BOB TURNED $2,684,354.56 INTO $5,368,709.12

It was raining in Dollarville, but it was a sunny day. Bob did not know what to think. However, the sun-shower created a perfect backdrop for a dream he both dreaded and longed to fulfill. He was worried and happy at the same time. His surprise gift idea was still safe, but this was an 'all hands-on deck' kind of morning...

Bob worked on the office buildings with Nelly, Ned, Mom, Dad, Aunt Sophia, Uncle Noah, and Uncle James. He even hired some contractors. This took up more of Bob's time as he had to manage more people, but he had a great team to help him out. When he needed to focus on schoolwork or anything else, his team would always back him up.

They all knew by now that success was no one person's journey, and as the saying goes, no man is an island. Bob ensured they had constant team-building activities to inspire unity and all the good stuff they needed. It wasn't all roses, but no matter what, they all ensured that the business came first.

He had to call Uncle Doubler for motivation sometimes.

"Be brave. Be strong. Be purposeful. Keep your spirits high," was one of his wisdom nuggets.

It took longer to get to the 29th day. Bob still had to deal with complicated financing, legal, tax, and insurance issues. Taxes are payments you make to the government for the things in your community, such as schools, roads, police officers, firefighters, and buildings. You pay taxes on the money you earn at work or the profit you make in a business. You also pay taxes if you own a house.

It was also Bob's final year in graduate school. His master's thesis was due. There were exams to take and papers to submit. He had to turn down the college parties.

Eventually, he sold the office buildings for a total of $5,368,709.12!

Bob called the team: Nelly, Ned, Mom, Dad, Aunt Sophia, Uncle Noah, and Uncle James. Together, they broke out into a little dance known as "The Twist." Dancing helped Bob reduce stiffness and pain. It was the ultimate therapy.

He had doubled his money again with the help of his family. He called the one person who helped him become the best he could be.

"Despite the challenges, you and your team pulled through. You are more than a business owner, Bob; you are a genuine leader," Uncle Doubler declared.

"And everyone on my team is also a leader," Bob replied with a smile. Uncle Doubler agreed.

While other students were roaming the streets or hanging out on the corner, Bob was out there hunting for deals, sniffing out cap rates, predicting profits, or rubbing shoulders with major real estate players in Dollarville.

Nothing excited him more than figuring out the values of some multifamily properties or scouting out other investment opportunities. Boring stuff! It was a little weird for some of his peers.

With some of the money, he bought Bond Street Apartments, one of the largest properties in Dollarville. He was sure to set aside something for the secret side project: Buying Mom a house with an enormous kitchen.

Bob had not given up his mission to promote economic empowerment in his community. In his mind, there should have been a program to support young business owners. Someone needed to teach the upcoming entrepreneurs how to start and grow their business. This time he wrote a letter to Congress. He wanted the legislative body to establish an Entrepreneurship Day in every school. He knew that all the kids studying science, technology, engineering, and math at Silverton University will depend on entrepreneurs to give them a job. Entrepreneurship was the engine that created jobs in Dollarville. Entrepreneurs were the job creators in the USA. There was no response.

Day 30

HOW BOB TURNED $5,368,709.12 INTO $10,737,418.24

The urge to prove doubters, naysayers and haters wrong threw Bob off the bed early. It was a powerful force. He felt that the time to watch the final poetic justice being served to his former classmate bullies was not far. But he was not sure if karma was ready to reveal her last hand. A million things could go wrong when dealing with an investment this big. He expected it to be a day from hell. What he didn't know was that it would also be the longest day in the world.

Bob quickly found out that fixing up and flipping an occupied apartment complex was a whole different ball game than flipping an empty house. It was the super bowl of flipping. He had to please the tenants and the potential real estate investors at the same time. It was challenging to complete renovations. It took forever to get the appropriate permits and inspections. Bob had to ensure that the contractors could work around the tenants' schedules and keep the disturbances to a minimum. Effective communication was required at every stage of the renovation.

He had to call Uncle Doubler several times for motivation. "Take it one step at a time. Don't let failure floor you."

Things became even more complicated when the time came to sell the property. Renters had their rights under the law. Showing occupied units to potential buyers was difficult. Bob had to work with the tenants, and some tenants felt frustrated and confused.

Bob was getting nervous and a little distressed about the situation. Things were not going well. For months, he was not getting reasonable offers. Bob had to keep the apartments occupied. It was more valuable to a real estate investor. He stood to sell it for a higher price. Also, the new tenants paid increased rental rates. That meant more money coming in.

He would walk the streets handing out flyers during the day to make sure people knew his apartments needed tenants. At night, he would do the marketing on social media.

There was a screening process for new tenants, requiring higher credit scores and higher income. Bad tenants could be a nuisance and a danger to the investment. Some of them were loud and abusive. There were also non-payers, deadbeats who avoided paying rent. Then some tenants complained constantly about every tiny little thing. Bob had to pay some current tenants to leave the complex.

He had to call Uncle Doubler again for some more wisdom nuggets and good vibes.

"You know the saying. It's always toughest just before you cross the finish line. Never give up. It only takes one offer," Uncle Doubler advised.

That was the push Bob needed to keep fighting. The good thing was that Bob had the right partners. He had Nelly, Ned, Mom, Dad, Aunt Sophia, Uncle Noah, and Uncle James. He had good contractors. He had learned how to network with brokers, bankers, leasing agents, realtors, and attorneys. He had hired very experienced real estate agents. The tenants were happy with the repairs and upgrades. Bob was starting to enjoy increased rental income from his investment when multiple generous offers came knocking. The first offer was huge, but the second one was even bigger. It was a sellers' market. Before he knew it, he was faced with multiple competing offers to purchase his property. He received more offers, all within hours of each other. Something else also happened. He received a fat official envelope from Dollarville city hall! His first inclination was to panic.

THE ORACLE OF THE COPPERS, THE APARTMENT COMPLEX

Bob was surprised by the sudden influx of buyers. It was apparent that he had a golden goose in his possession. In recent years, most of the vacant land in Denver City had been overtaken by city blocks of new residential and commercial buildings. It was too expensive for investors. There was little inventory on the market. Heading east to Dollarville was the best option. Located just a view block from the historic Dollarville Rail Depot, the newly renovated Apartment Complex suddenly attracted investors. It was hard to find such a historic spot that is still near a major metropolis. The majestic views of the Rockies added to the charm. That the snow-capped mountains can be seen in the distance made it even more valuable.

Bob knew that a rental property can be a great source of passive income. The apartment complex would create jobs for his family and other people in the city. That made him develop a severe case of seller's remorse. Bob no longer wanted to sell the complex. A state-of-the-art sign at the property's main gate that read "Copper Oracle Apartments" made it harder for him to part with it. He came up with a different idea. With the money from the rents, he planned to get more income-producing assets.

Bob wanted to retire his parents. But they wanted to work, so he requested his parents quit their jobs and work with him. Dad did not hesitate to take the offer. He was suffering from chronic back, neck, and joint pain. The physical tasks at the railroad yard were becoming unbearable. The pounding his body absorbed after two decades as a track laborer had taken its toll. Dad quickly left the backbreaking rail yard job and became the property manager.

Mom also made the decision to quit her job to become the front desk receptionist. She would no longer be ringing up sales at the grocery store cash register. She would collect rent and handling tenant issues instead.

Ned and Nelly became maintenance technicians. After pleading with their little brother to provide them with housing, each of them received a rent-free apartment. Bob had no choice. His sanity depended on how the family healed from past pain and trauma. He would do anything not to trigger the old wounds and unresolved issues. Bob recalled how he was vulnerable to physical and verbal abuse as the youngest child because of his role within the family. His life depended on his dysfunctional family. But now, he had a new role of caring for his older siblings. He did not want anyone in the family relying on crime to bring in an income. Copper Oracle Apartments became home to Ned and Nelly.

Bob could not help but secretly enjoy the "I told you so" moment.

"Didn't I tell you two that one day you will beg to live in my dreams?" he thought.

An acorn had become an oak tree. What had started as a silly dream was now a family-owned and operated real estate business. Copper Oracle Apartments required 20 more employees right away. People rushed in to fill the open positions in the complex. The applicants included the schoolmates who had derided him back in the day. It brought back memories of distressing experiences from the past. What they did was still raw and painful to him.

"The audacity!" he thought. But victory tastes so much sweeter after failure. It was incredible to see all those doubters and naysayers lining up for job applications. Bob felt intense bitterness welling up, but there was no need for revenge. Karma was working its magic quite well.

Bob had a forgiving heart. He never wanted to dwell in a tit-for-tat mindset. After all, he had overcome cruelty, mocking, and insults from people who thought he was crazy, and he was no longer a laughingstock. The bold young man had become a kind of hero of his time. As a matter of fact, he had become a symbol of possibility and hope to others. He was the city's best example of working hard, investing wisely, and creating generational wealth.

What about doubling the shiny penny? Bob hired commercial appraisers to estimate the value of the apartment complex. Bob waited for the decision with fingers crossed. He wanted to know his net worth.

After getting the appraisal of Copper Oracle Apartments, he started the calculations. Bob calculated his net worth by deducting the value of all his liabilities from the value of his assets. Assets included anything of value that he owned that can be converted into cash. Liabilities, on the other hand, represented his debts or what he needed to pay off.

"This can't be right," he thought. He had to check his numbers twice. His net worth was more than $10,737,418.24.

He had doubled his money, again. Ten million dollars! It had only taken 30 days. "Ten million dollars!" Uncle Doubler could not believe it.

Uncle Doubler was pleased to hear that Bob was thinking about other income-producing investments. He knew the importance of sustainable business growth. Uncle Doubler was a talented financial advisor and a fastidious investor. He advised Bob to diversify his new investments. That way, Bob wouldn't suffer too great a loss if one investment did poorly. Diversification means putting money into different investments. Instead of putting all his money on buildings, Bob could invest some in stocks, bonds, and interest-bearing savings accounts.

"Don't put all your eggs in one basket, son," Uncle Doubler advised.

Bob liked the idea. He always wanted to own big companies. A stock is a piece of a company. When you own a stock of a company, you own a small part of it. Some stocks also pay dividends. What is that? A dividend is a payment from a company to its stockholders. Let's say Bob has 1,000 shares of stock in a company that pays an annual dividend of $1. He would receive $1,000 in dividends during the year. Bob was excited. He was about to be the proud owner of a big company or two! Well, at least a small piece of it.

It was time to present his family with a gift of a lifetime. Mom was half-crying, half-celebrating when she got the keys. 316 John Street was one of the best houses in the city. Mom could not believe her eyes. She had an enormous kitchen with white cabinets, stainless steel appliances, and a large granite-topped island in the center. She was treated to views of Mount Evans, Pikes Peak, Mount Bierstadt, and Torreys Peak just by opening the blinds.

"They say, "A river that forgets its source will eventually dry up,""" Mom sobbed with joy. "Thank you for not forgetting your mama."

Mom was also quick to give her new address to her church friends.

"John 3:16!" she shouted with joy. She found the biblical reference both amusing and satisfying. Deep down, she also knew that it was a miracle that her children could patch up their rough relationships. Few parents were that lucky.

Bob did not forget to treat himself. He settled on Wall Street, quite a few blocks away from Maple Avenue. Wall Street ran between Mountain View Road in the west and the Silver Run River in the east of Dollarville. It was a happy place with a spectacular view of Denver's skyline. His new backyard featured the incredible views of the Rockies and the Front Range.

It turned out the fat official envelope was directly from the Mayor of Dollarville, Mr. Rich Rand. There was no reason to panic. The mayor wanted to organize an enormous party to celebrate Bob for making a positive difference in the community. On top of developing the city and creating jobs, Bob had donated money to local charities. He had also sponsored an entrepreneurship and financial literacy program in all local schools. He did not want other kids to grow up without learning how to earn, save, and invest. He believed children should not be kept in the dark about personal finance topics. He wanted to take his message to children all over the country, inspiring them to follow their dreams and showing them how to be excellent money managers.

When the day of the party came, everyone was all smiles. The entire city showed up. The arrival of students and teachers caused a great stir. Hamilton Elementary School, Washington Middle School, Prospect High School, and even Silverton University were well represented! Bob made sure the "Young Entrepreneurs Club" members got front-row seats.

While guests made themselves comfortable, Bob was in a sort of silent prayer. He was nervous. The thought of public speaking sent sweat pouring from his pores and brought a sick feeling to his gut. It was not his cup of tea.

The mayor took the microphone to introduce the occasion. In an emotional speech, the mayor praised Bob's commitment to the city. He was fully aware that no one else in the room had a net worth that was remotely close to Bob's. He was also quick to praise Bob's parents for raising him well. He knew the Benjamins worked hard to bring home the bacon for their children. He wanted the family to stay in the city. In a turn of events, he accepted Bob's idea to introduce a day to celebrate entrepreneurship in the city. Just like that, Dollarville Entrepreneurship Day was born.

Bob was delighted to have his letter-writing campaign finally recognized, but being feted as a job creator was just the icing on the cake. Everyone was on their feet as Bob was presented with the key to the city. Then the mayor handed him the dreaded hot mic. It was the worst part of the festival. He appeared calm, but he was dying inside. No one knew he was just putting on a brave face. The paralyzing fear and panic were almost unbearable.

After thanking the Mayor, Bob gushed with gratitude for all the people who had supported him through the journey.

"I want to give a shout-out to Mom, Dad, Ned, Nelly, Uncle Noah, Uncle James, and Aunt Sophia. You guys are the best," he said, his voice cracking with emotion.

Bob continued as people kept on clapping and shouting, "Bravo!" He had special thanks for Uncle Doubler, for his mentorship over the years. "I can still hear your voice, Uncle, saying, 'Go out there, son. Stay out of debt. Buy low! Sell high! Earn! Save! Invest! Repeat!'"

Bob quickly raised his glass, ready to exit the stage.

"To the dusty demolition days!" He shouted, referring to the days they all spent covered in construction dirt, dust, sweat, and paint.

He was not used to everyone staring at him in envy! Most grown-ups in the room would probably never reach their 30th doubling day.

But the mayor grabbed him back. "What lessons did you learn?"

"This has been an eye-opening journey. I now have a great appreciation for people who build things and bring us stuff in trucks, cables, pipes, and airwaves. I mean people who perform trades behind the scenes, like the electricians, carpenters, joiners, plumbers, painters, motor mechanics, bricklayers, landscapers, terminators, and waste haulers. The truck drivers. The rail track laborers like my dad here. I salute you. I am convinced that you are the most essential people in modern civilization. I have seen you brave a minus-30 wind-chill. Without you, the world would be quite a different place. It was an honor working with you." Bob became emotional as the crowd cheered.

Bob thought he was done, but the mayor grabbed his hand again. "Bob, say something to the youth, really quick. What's the secret?" the mayor insisted. Deep down, the mayor knew it was not just the young people who needed financial advice. Most Dollarville's residents were still stuck somewhere between Day 1 and Day 27.

Bob took the floor again.

"I don't know what to say. There is no secret, my friends. Work hard and study hard. Sometimes what you don't do with your money maybe even more important than what you do with it. Don't spend to impress others. Don't spend on things you don't need. Wealth is a byproduct of time and money. Start investing as early as possible. The sooner you understand money, the sooner you can make more of it. Investing is all about spotting potential and taking calculated risks. As Uncle Doubler would say, "Don't live in fear but don't be cavalier." A job allows you to work for money. An investment allows money to work for you. And this is a big one, find a mentor. I wouldn't be standing here today if I didn't have Uncle Doubler. Every kid needs someone to provide advice, support, or even just listen to him. Every child deserves an experienced and trusted adviser."

Bob was quick to dish his own nuggets of wisdom.

"Finally, and most importantly, find what makes you happy. Success is not measured only by money and things. Wealth, positions, or fame are not guarantees of happiness. Find time to make a positive

116

difference in your community. Find time to laugh, make friends, and dance. I love investing, but I am still the dancing kid.

And on that note, Mr. DJ, hit it!" Bob concluded as the pulsating beats took over the airwaves. It was time for the DJ to spin a mix of oldies.

"Come on, everybody, clap your hands," Bob shouted as he led the dance. His brothers, parents, uncles and aunt joined him at the front. This was Bob's favorite part of the day. It was time to cast all his cares on the dance floor. He was no longer tense, even in front of the crowd. Dancing enabled him to be in the moment. It transported him to a higher dimension.

There was another miracle. With no warning, the nerdy chairman of the "Young Entrepreneurs Club" and company invaded the floor. This one was for the history books. No one had ever seen them cut a rug, even accidentally.

"Pigs have flown, and hell has frozen over!" Nelly quipped over the rhythm-heavy music.

Finally, everyone was popping, locking, dropping, freestyling, and all other manners of getting down. Then the best moment happened. The crowd was able to synchronize into a set of catchy movements.

They broke into a little dance known as "Cha Cha Slide," moving freely and joyfully to the beats as the distant snowy peaks faded into night.

THE END

GLOSSARY

401(k)

A 401(k) is a long-term savings account sponsored by the employer, which you don't touch until you retire. Most people retire at age 59.5 or older.

Example: John puts $1,000 every month in his 401(k). When he retires, John will have all the money he put away to save for retirement. This way, he doesn't have to work or worry about money when he is retired.

Asset

An asset is anything of value that you own. Examples: Cash, stocks, bonds, cars, houses.

Bonds

Bonds are investments in debt. When you buy a bond, you're lending that company money. In other words, a bond is a loan to a company or government that pays investors back with interest.

Examples: U.S. Treasury bonds, corporate bonds, municipal bonds.

Budget

A budget is like a map for your money. It tells you what you need to pay, where your money goes, and how much you have left each month.

Example: Joe created a monthly budget to know if he had enough money for his bills, groceries, gas, and entertainment.

Cash Flow

The net amount of cash being transferred into and out of a business.

Compound Interest

When you put money in a savings account, the money earns interest. If you leave the original money plus the interest you earned in the bank, your interest earns interest, known as compound interest.

Example: Let's say you put $100 in a savings account, and each year it earns a 10% return. You earn $10 in interest that year. If you leave that $110 in the savings account, it will earn $11 interest the following year. This will keep going or compounding until you withdraw the funds if you leave that $121 in the savings account.

Credit Score

A credit score is like grades on your report card, but for your finances. If you pay your bills on time, you get a 'good grade.' If you don't pay your bills on time, you get a 'poor grade.' Credit scores range from 300 to 850. The higher your score, the better credit you have.

Example: John has a 650-credit score, and Bella has an 800-credit score. Bella will have an easier time getting a bank loan when she needs it because she has a higher credit score or a 'better grade.'

Debt

Debt is money you borrow you must pay back.

Example: A few examples of debt are a car loan, house loan, or credit card. They are all borrowed funds you must pay back each month.

Demand

Demand is how badly people want a good or a service. If people want your product and are willing to part with their hard-earned money for it, we say there is demand.

Diversification

Diversification means spreading the risk of loss using different investments. We avoid putting all our eggs in one basket.

Dividend

A dividend is a payment from a company to its stockholders. The company decides each time how much it will pay per share.

Example: The XYZ Company issues a $2 dividend per share. If you own 100 shares, you will get $200.

Earning

Earning is what you do when you work. You get paid to have a job; that's your earnings.

Example: Joe has a job at the local hardware store. He makes $15 per hour. If Joe works 5 hours, he has $75 in earnings that day.

Emergency Fund

An emergency fund is a stash of money set aside to cover the financial surprises life throws your way. Examples of emergencies are job loss, medical or dental emergency, unexpected home repairs, car troubles, unplanned travel expenses.

Entrepreneur

An entrepreneur is someone who starts a business. Sometimes they have a new idea to start something or start a service that already exists, but they know they can provide it too.

Example: If you are good at mowing lawns, you may start a lawn-mowing business. You would charge people for your services to mow their lawn.

Expenses

Amounts of money spent to buy goods and services for yourself or your business. In other words, the money going out.

Generational Wealth

Generational wealth represents assets passed down from one generation to the next. These assets can include real estate, stock market investments, a business, or anything else that contains a monetary value.

Giving

Giving occurs when you give someone money, such as a charity. This is also known as donating. You are spending the money, but it's a charitable gift.

Example: You are driving down the street and see a woman collecting money for the Cancer Society. You put $1 in her bucket. You gave or donated $1.

Good

A good is something that you can use or consume, like food or toys or books or car or clothes. Goods are tangible items. They can be seen or touched.

Identity Theft

You have your own identity and social security number. If a thief gets a hold of your information, he/she steals your identity and may use it. This is illegal.

Example: A criminal gets a hold of your name and social security number. They use it to open a new credit card in your name. This is identity theft.

Income

Money earned through employment and investments.

Insurance

Insurance is something people buy to protect themselves from losing money. The insurance company promises it will pay a certain amount of money to cover expenses if an accident happens or a family member gets sick.

Interest

Interest is either money you are paid for lending your money or an amount of money added to the money you borrowed. Interest is what you pay the bank to borrow the money. If you are the person lending the money, you earn the interest for lending the money.

Example: You pay interest on a car loan when you borrow money from the bank to buy a car. The interest is added to the amount you owe each month.

When you put your money in a savings account, you lend the bank your money. The bank then pays you the interest to keep your money.

Inventory

Inventory is the items that your business has bought, intending to resell to customers.

Investment

Investment means buying an asset, such as a stock, that you think will be worth more when selling it. Investing means putting money into assets (like stocks, bonds, mutual funds, real estate, etc.) to help you reach your financial goals.

Liability

A liability is any debts or payments you owe to someone else. Examples: Credit card debt, car loan.

Loan

A loan is a form of debt. You borrow money from a bank and must make monthly payments to pay the debt back. You pay interest on the loan; this is the charge for borrowing the money.

Example: You can borrow money to buy a car or a house. The bank gives you the money, and you pay the loan back each month.

Mutual Fund

A mutual fund is a basket of individual stocks. Instead of picking out individual stocks on your own, you can buy a mutual fund.

Need

A need is something you must have to survive, like food, water, and a home.

Needs vs. Wants

You have to divide your money between needs and wants.

Example: John's mom has to pay the bills. She has the house payment and the electricity bill. Those are needs. Without a house or electricity, it would be hard to live. John's mom has little money to pay for John's new toy that he wants. John has toys, but he would like a new one – that's a want.

Net Worth

Your net worth is your assets minus your debts. Net worth = assets – liabilities

Opportunity Cost

Opportunity cost is the value of the next best thing you give up whenever you make a decision. Whenever you make a trade-off, the thing that you do not choose is your opportunity cost. Any time you buy something, you're sacrificing the ability to spend that money on something else. The cost of something is what you will give up to get it. It can be money, time, or some other resource.

Profit

Profit is the money that is left after expenses have been paid. It is what you get when you sell something for a higher price than you paid for it. That's why businesses set prices for their items. They charge customers more than they paid to get the items so they can earn a profit.

Example: If you set up a lemonade stand and it costs you $10, you would want to make more than $10 to have a profit or more money in your pocket. If you don't sell enough lemonade to make more than $10, it's called a loss. Breaking even is when the money coming in is equal to the money going out. There is no profit or loss.

Real Estate

An area of land, including the trees, water, and buildings on it. Think of real estate as the property, land, buildings, and air rights above the land and underground rights below the land.

Risk

Risk is the possibility or chance of loss. When investing, there is always a likelihood that you could lose some or all your investment.

Therefore, we need to diversify our investments. The key to investing is to minimize the risk and maximize the financial reward. Only invest what you can afford to lose.

Saving

Saving means putting some of the money you earned aside in an account that you don't touch.

Example: Joe's paycheck was $1,000. He put $100 of that money in his savings account so that he wouldn't touch it. The following month he added another $100 to it, so now he has $200 in his savings account.

Service

A service is something that someone does for you, like giving you a haircut or making you dinner or even teaching you social studies. Services are intangible items. They cannot be seen or touched.

Spending

When you spend money, you pay money for goods or services. Controlling your expenses can help you achieve the goal of saving and investing more money each year. You don't have to give up everything you enjoy; just cut back little by little.

Example: When you go to the store to buy a pack of gum, you spend money on the gum. Let's say the gum is $1. You pay the cashier $1, so you spent $1.

Stock

When you buy a stock, you buy a part of the company. Stocks are an investment.

Example: You buy stock in XYZ Company. Let's say you buy 2 shares. You own 2 shares of XYZ Company. You can keep the stock or sell it to someone else, which you typically do when the stock prices go up.

Supply

Supply is the amount of a good or service that producers are willing and able to supply at a specific price.

Taxes

Taxes are payments you make to the government in exchange for the things in your community, such as schools, roads, police officers, firefighters, and buildings.

Example: You pay taxes on the money you earn at work. You also pay taxes if you own a house.

Trade-off

Sacrificing one thing to obtain another is called a trade-off. We can decide whether to save or spend our money now. We can decide whether to study or go have some fun.

Want

A want is something nice to have, but you can live without it, like ice cream or a toy.

ABOUT THE AUTHOR

Author Mahugu Nuthu, B.Sc. M.Sc. a passionate campaigner for financial literacy for kids, is a research analyst with years of experience in the financial services industry. He obtained his Masters of Science in Accounting degree from Kean University in New Jersey

Bobs Money Doubling Challenge

START		0.01
Day	1	0.02
Day	2	0.04
Day	3	0.08
Day	4	0.16
Day	5	0.32
Day	6	0.64
Day	7	1.28
Day	8	2.56
Day	9	5.12
Day	10	10.24
Day	11	20.48
Day	12	40.96
Day	13	81.92
Day	14	163.84
Day	15	327.68
Day	16	655.36
Day	17	1,310.72
Day	18	2,621.44
Day	19	5,242.88
Day	20	10,485.76
Day	21	20,971.52
Day	22	41,943.04
Day	23	83,886.08
Day	24	167,772.16
Day	25	335,544.32
Day	26	671,088.64
Day	27	1,342,177.28
Day	28	2,684,354.56
Day	29	5,368,709.12
Day	30	10,737,418.24

Profit and Loss		
Profit And Loss Report		
Sales (Revenue)	24	Bob sold 24 bottles of water for $1 each
Cost of Goods Sold	10.24	Bob had bought these 24 bottles of water for $10.24 from a superstore
Gross Profit	13.76	Gross Profit = Revenue – Cost of Goods Sold
Expenses	3.52	Bob spent some of the profits at the game
Net Income	10.24	Net Income = Gross Profit - Expenses

Guide to Writing a Simple Business Plan		
Business Name	What is the name of your business? What does this name say about your business?	
Business Idea	What is your big idea? Is it a product or a service?	
The problem	What is the need for your product or service?	
The solution	How does your product or service and how it solves the problem?	
Competitive advantage	What is your competition? What makes your idea unique or better? Why will people buy it?	
Business model	How will you make money (profit)?	
Customers	Who is your customer and how many of them are out there?	
Market	Where will you sell your product or service?	
Promotion	How will you get the word out about your business?	
Risks	What could derail your business plan?	
Regulations	What regulations do you need to comply with?	
Start Costs	How much will it cost to start your business?	
Funding	Where will you get the money to cover your startup costs?	
Cost per Unit	What is the cost of making each product or providing each hour of service?	
Pricing	How much will you charge?	
Profit	What will be your profit?	
Financial goals	What will you do with the money you make?	

Notes

Doubling Day No.		

Date	Week Of:	Year:

Today, I am grateful for...	Today would be great if...

I AM affirmation.		
	Opening Balance	
	Sales (Revenue)	
	Cost of Goods Sold	
	Gross Profit	
	Expenses	
	Net Income	

Today's Big Idea (Product or a Service)	Closing Balance	
	Notes/Reminders	

To Do List

- ☐
- ☐
- ☐
- ☐
- ☐
- ☐
- ☐
- ☐
- ☐
- ☐
- ☐

ALSO AVAILABLE

30-Day Business Planner For Kids

Designed with a mission to empower kids through financial literacy, this 30-page journal guides kids through a powerful goal-setting and daily business planning process.

The page-a-day entries are perfect for kids to keep track of their journey with easy-to-understand financial tips. Its not just essential to their growth it is a good way for kids to exercise their entrepreneurial spirit, learn to set goals and pursue their passion.

A perfect gift for that entrepreneurial kid in your life who loves to earn, save and invest. It's a great birthday, holiday, start of the season or back to school gift for kids. This planner is also great for business mentors and organizations as part of a financial literacy campaign. It's the ultimate tool for school teachers and counselors if used as part of a business curriculum.

What's inside?

Guide on how to create a simple business plan.
Guide on how to prepare a simple Profit And Loss Report
Penny Doubling Challenge
30-Day Daily Journal
Daily Journal Entry Pages
Today, I am grateful for...
Today would be great if...
I AM affirmation..
Product or a Service
Opening balance
 Sales (Revenue)
Cost of Goods Sold
Gross Profit
Expenses
Net Income
Closing balance
I AM affirmation..
To do list
Notes/Reminders

What ages is this journal good for?
We recommend ages 8 - 13.

www.ingramcontent.com/pod-product-compliance
Lightning Source LLC
Chambersburg PA
CBHW071924220626
47052CB00002B/450